Collins

need to know?

Chess

Tony Gillam

Collins

First published in 2006 by Collins
an imprint of
HarperCollins Publishers
77-85 Fulham Palace Road
London W6 8JB

www.collins.co.uk

A catalogue record for this book is available from the British Library

Created by: m&n publishing
Editor: Nina Sharman
Designer: Martin Hendry
Series design: Mark Thomson
Front cover photograph: © Getty Images
Back cover photographs: © Corbis
Photograph on page9 by permission of the British Library

ISBN-10: 0-00-720595-3
ISBN-13: 978-0-00-720595-0

Colour reproduction by Colourscan, Singapore
Printed and bound by Printing Express Ltd, Hong Kong

Contents

1 **Getting started** 6

2 **Next moves** 66

3 **Winning pieces** 82

4 **Some simple games** 108

5 **Ways to avoid losses** 126

6 **More ideas** 138

7 **Leading players** 158

Glossary 182

Need to know more? 187

Index 190

Acknowledgements 191

1 Getting started

Chess is one of the most widely played games on earth. It is also one of the oldest and is still going strong, having kept people fascinated over thousands of years. This is your chance to find out just what it is about chess that has captivated so many but be warned, once this game has you in its grip, it will never let you go. In this chapter you will learn about the fundamental aspects of the game – the chess board, the pieces and the moves.

The birth of chess

The first written evidence of a game resembling chess appears in about AD 600 in Indian writings, but some historians believe that chess goes back several thousand years before that date.

ABOVE: An illustration from *The Game and Playe of the Chesse*. The board has the correct number of squares but it is the wrong way round (see page 13). Notice too that the king is allowed to sit when playing but his opponent is not.

OPPOSITE: A miniature painting, dated 1437, from a manuscript of an epic poem, entitled Shahnama. The illustration depicts the Kayd of Hind in India presenting Anushirvan with a chess set.

Origins of the game

Chess almost certainly began in what is today India and developed from a game that was a battle between two armies, both led by their king. The moves and names of the chess pieces have changed over the centuries but there is enough information available to make it possible to follow the game's development over the last 1,400 years.

Chess was keenly played in the Arab World towards the end of the first millennium. The earliest manuscripts on chess that we have date from that time and we even know the names of some of their best players.

The first chess book to appear in the English language was *The Game and Playe of the Chesse* (probably in 1476), which was reprinted in 1480 and a number of times since then up until the 1970s. This was one of the first books to be printed in the English language.

The coming of chess books was an important development in the game as, not only did books spread knowledge, but they also helped to fix the rules by eliminating local methods of play.

'About 1500' is the date generally given for the beginning of modern chess; however, there wasn't final agreement on the rules until *c.*1880.

Buying a chess set and board

There is a huge range of sets and boards on the market, which come in many sizes and styles, so a word of advice on what to buy and where to buy it may be helpful.

Choosing and using

If you are intending to play with the set, as opposed to looking at it or displaying it, then you should avoid the various ornate ones that are for sale in gift shops. Some decorative pieces tend to break easily and are not suitable for regular use.

Chess sets are made in a variety of materials, most commonly in wood or plastic, and are sold according to the height of the king. Most competitive chess is played with kings that measure 75–90mm (3–3½in) high. Plastic sets are less expensive, more durable and easier to clean. It is

BELOW: An attractive, traditional chess set and board ready for the start of a game. Wooden sets like this were used for hundreds of years but most competitive games are now played with plastic pieces.

LEFT: Wooden boards are usually brown and cream. These colours are softer on the eye than black and white but they also need brown and cream chess pieces to look right.

best to avoid coloured sets where it isn't clear which side is black and which is white.

It is also possible to buy sets that are 'felted' and 'weighted'. Both of these extras add to the price a little but you may consider it to be worth it. A 'felted' set has felt on the bottom of the pieces to make moving them quieter (this is more important if you are using a wooden board than a plastic one). 'Weighting' is the name given when lead is inserted into the bottom of the pieces in order to make them heavier and so harder to knock over.

Wooden boards are expensive. They can cost more than the set! Competitive chess is often played with a plastic board that can be rolled up for carrying about and wiped clean. There are also better quality plastic boards that are more rigid.

Pieces with 75mm (3in) kings require a board with 45mm (1¾in) squares; sets with 95mm (3¾in) kings should have a board with 50mm (2in) squares.

ABOVE: These two wooden pieces are 'weighted' with lead that would have been inserted into the bases prior to them being covered over by felt.

ABOVE: This computerised chess set is useful if you wish to practice your skills and you have no opponent. However, today many people have access to a computer, which offers a similar opportunity.

It's a good idea to start with something that is not too costly; if you enjoy the game and intend to keep playing, you can consider something more expensive at a later date. When buying a set, check to see if it comes in a bag or a box. If not, it is worth buying a plastic box with a lid that snaps shut, rather like a food container.

For a wide selection of boards and sets, at the most competitive prices, buy from a specialist chess dealer – take a look on the internet. Unless you intend to play competitive chess, it is not necessary to buy a chess clock (this is used to time the moves of both you and your opponent). They are expensive and you simply do not need one.

Getting to know the board

A chess board is divided up into 64 equally sized squares that are alternately coloured light and dark (white and black). The boards commonly used are between 40 and 56 cm (16 and 22 in) square.

Columns, rows and colours

The vertical columns of squares running from player to player (or top to bottom) are called 'files'. The horizontal rows running from left to right are called 'ranks'. 'Diagonals' are straight lines of squares that are the same colour.

No matter what the colours of the chess pieces in your set are, the light coloured pieces are always called 'white' and the dark coloured pieces are always called 'black'.

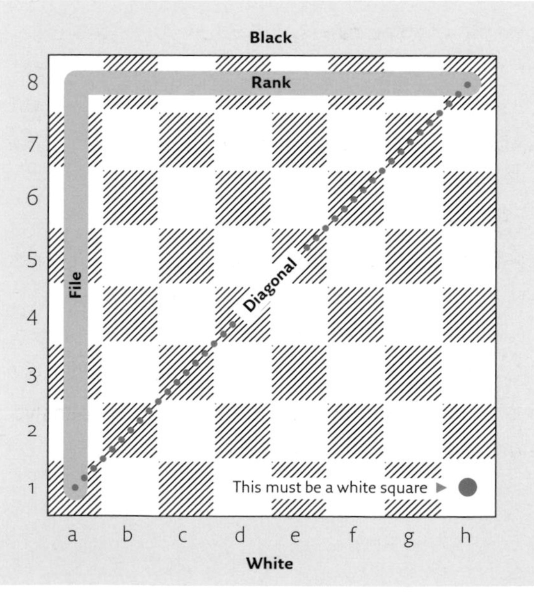

must know

Board direction

In nearly all diagrams in chess books, including this book, White is shown playing up the board and Black plays down the board.

▶ **Right way round** For a proper game of chess to be played, the board **must** be placed so that there is a white square in the bottom right hand corner – follow the rhyme 'White on the right'. Getting the board the wrong way round is a very common mistake.

must know

First moves
In every chess game, White makes the first move. Next Black makes a move and then White makes a second move and so on. When it is your turn, you **must** move. No 'passing' is allowed. You can **never** have more than one piece on the same square at the same time.

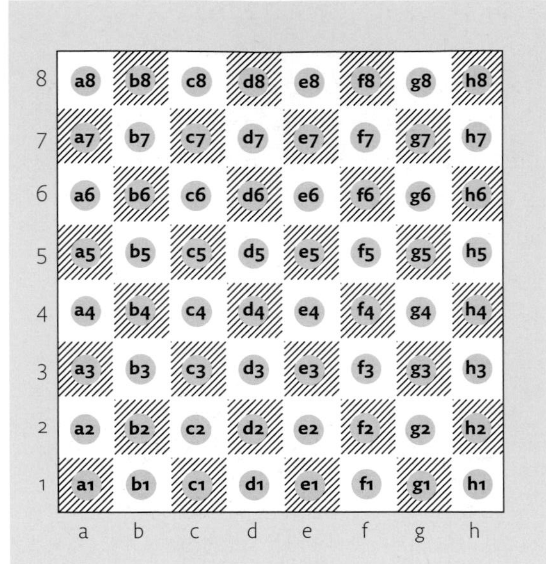

The names of the squares

Every square has a name, making it easy to write down any chess move (see page 72). The files (vertical columns) are lettered a–h, from left to right. The ranks (horizontal rows) are numbered 1–8, from White's side of the board. When referring to a square the file is noted first, followed by the rank.

For example, the queens begin the game on squares d1 and d8 and the kings begin on e1 and e8 (see the diagram opposite).

The white pawns begin on the second rank, squares a2 to h2, and the black pawns on the seventh rank, squares a7 to h7 (see the diagram opposite).

Setting up a chessboard

Each side has 16 pieces – eight pawns, two rooks, two bishops, two knights, one queen and one king.

When you set out the pieces on the board, make sure that you place the queens on their own colour squares – the white queen on a white square and the black queen on a black square.

As you can see in the diagram below, the queens start on the d-file and the kings on the e-file.

did you know?

Walk tall
The two tallest pieces in every chess set are always the kings.

Symmetry of pieces
Note that both sides have a rook on the a- and h-files; a knight on the b- and g-files and a bishop on the c- and f-files.

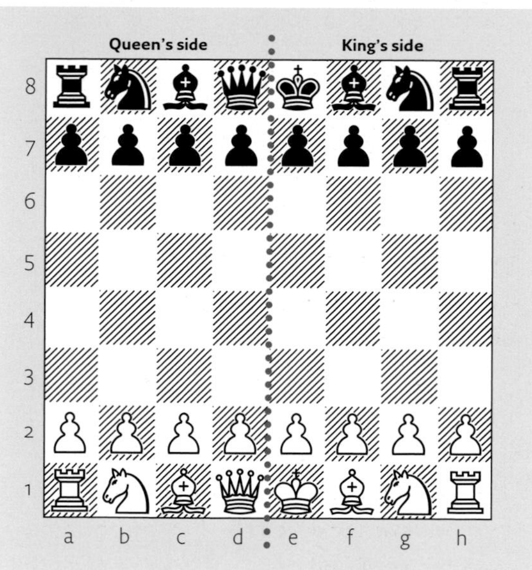

the chess pieces

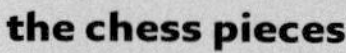

Pawn
See pages 16–24

Rook
See pages 30–4

Knight
See pages 40–5

Bishop
See pages 25–9

Queen
See pages 35–9

King
See pages 46–50

The pawn

Pawns are the equivalent of foot soldiers in an army. Foot soldiers are expected to advance towards the enemy and not to retreat, so pawns cannot move backwards.

The weakest link

The pawns are the smallest and weakest of the chess pieces. White pawns start on squares a2–h2; black pawns on squares a7–h7. Each side has eight pawns and below the photograph you can see how they appear in the diagrams in this book.

How pawns move

Pawns may only move straight down a file. They may move one or two squares (your choice) on their first move but, after that, only one square at a time.

The white pawn on b2 can move to b3 or b4 (because this is its first move), but after this move it can only advance one square at a time. The black pawn on d5 can only move to d4 (because it has already moved, it may only advance one square at a time). The pawn at f2 can move to f3 or f4 and the pawn at h6 may only advance to h5.

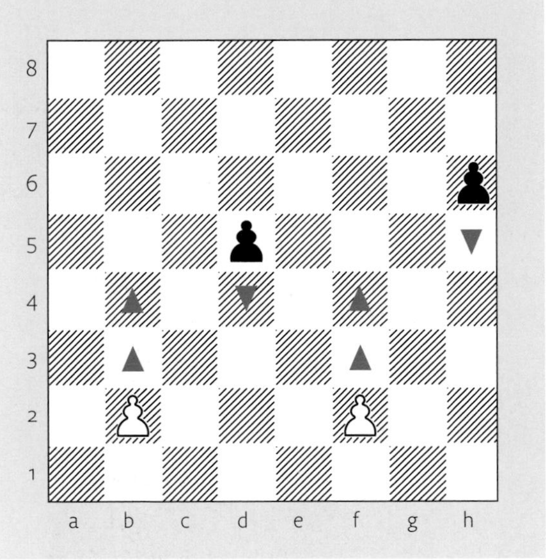

must know

Forwards only
Pawns cannot move backwards and they cannot jump over another piece.

must know

Capture and attack

▶ When you take an opponent's piece you are said to 'capture' it. You choose whether or not to capture. You are not obliged to capture if you don't want to. This is true for all pieces, not just pawns.

▶ When a piece is threatened by an enemy piece , it is said to be 'attacked'.

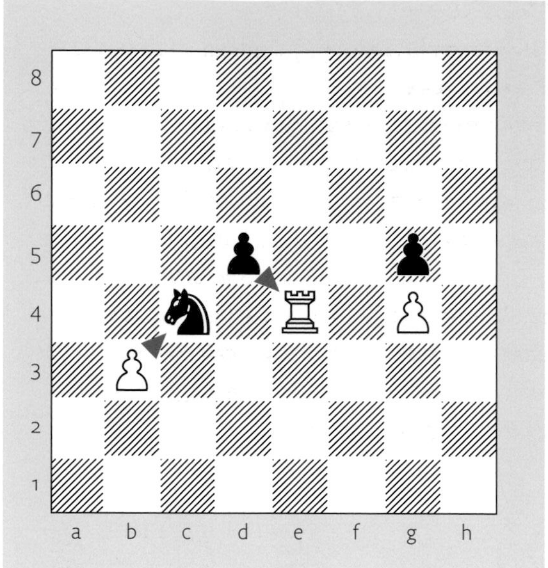

How pawns capture

Pawns may only capture other pieces by moving diagonally one square.

In the above diagram, if it is White to move, then the white pawn on b3 may capture the black knight on c4. This is done by picking up the pawn from b3 and putting it on c4 and removing the knight. If it is Black to move, then the black pawn on d5 could take the white rook on e4. The pawns on g4 and g5 block one another. Neither can move forwards nor can they capture.

Pawns can usually attack two squares. For example, the b3 white pawn attacks squares a4 and c4 and the g4 white pawn attacks f5 and h5.

Which four squares do the black pawns attack?

The d5-pawn attacks c4 (so it defends the knight) and e4. The g5-pawn attacks f4 and h4.

Practice with pawns

What moves and captures can each of the pawns make?

In this example, the a2-pawn can move to a3 or a4 (but cannot capture). The c3-pawn can move to c4 or capture the black knight on d4. The e2-pawn and g4-pawn cannot move or capture at the moment.

The a7-pawn can move to a6 or a5, or capture the bishop on b6. The c5-pawn can move to c4 but cannot capture. The e4-pawn can do nothing. The g5-pawn can capture the white knight on f4 but cannot otherwise move .

must know

Recap on the pawn

Pawns can only move straight forwards along their file. They can never move backwards. Pawns can only capture diagonally one square.

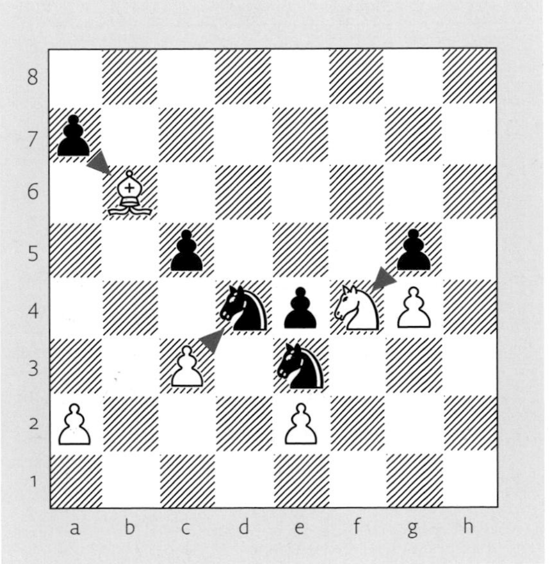

Which two pawns can only attack one square each and why?

The a2-pawn can only attack b3, and the a7-pawn can only attack b6. This is because they are positioned at the side of the board.

good to know

Defenders

A piece is defended if, should it be captured, the capturing piece can itself be taken.

Excercises with pawns

What moves and captures can each of the white pawns make?

The b4- and b5-pawns cannot advance. The b5-pawn cannot capture, however, the b4-pawn can take the black pawn on c5. The e4-pawn can move to e5 or take the black pawn on f5. The f3-pawn can move to f4 or take the black pawn on g4. The g2-pawn can move to g3 but cannot capture.

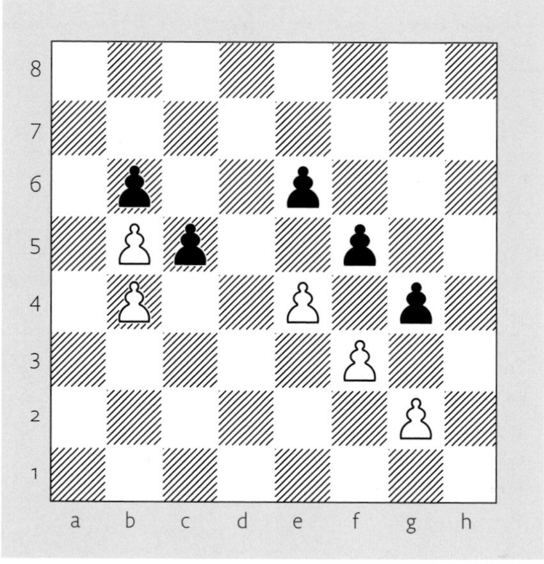

What moves and captures can each of the black pawns make?

The b6-pawn cannot move or capture. The c5-pawn can move to c4 or take the white pawn on b4. The e6-pawn can move to e5 but cannot capture. The f5-pawn can move to f4 or capture the white pawn on e4. The g4-pawn can move to g3 or capture the white pawn on f3.

Pawns are good defenders

In the diagram opposite there are ten pawns, five of them are defended or protected and five aren't.

The pawn on c5 is defended because, if White takes it with the b4-pawn, Black can then recapture with the b6-pawn. The f5-pawn is also defended because if White captures it with the e4-pawn, Black can then recapture with the e6-pawn.

If White takes the g4-pawn with the f3-pawn, then Black can recapture with his f5-pawn.

If Black takes the white pawn on e4, the f3-pawn can recapture, and if Black takes the white pawn on f3, then the g2-pawn can recapture.

The b5, g2, b6 and e6 pawns are not defended, but at the same time they are not under attack. The b4-pawn is not defended but it is attacked by the c5-pawn.

watch out!

Your targets

Keep your own pieces defended and keep an eye open for any of your opponent's pieces that are not protected. These are the ones to try to capture, because your opponent cannot recapture!

good to know

Pawns as defenders

The pawn makes a very good defender because it is the lowest value piece (see page 68). Try to use your stronger pieces to attack with, not for defending.

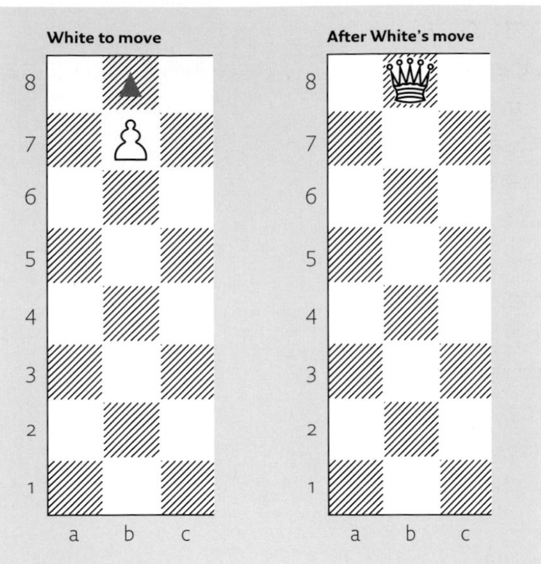

Pawn promotion

Sometimes a pawn can become a much more important piece. This happens when a pawn reaches the far end of the board and is immediately promoted to, or transformed into, a knight, bishop, rook or queen (your choice). Most players choose a queen because it is the most powerful piece (see page 68).

Promotion happens in one move as in these two examples.

must know

From pawn to queen
Even if you still have your first queen on the board, you are allowed to promote a pawn to make another queen. Either use a queen from another chess set or, if you don't have another set, use a coin - but remember it is a queen. In theory, you could have lots of queens, but you should be able to win the game without promoting very many pawns.

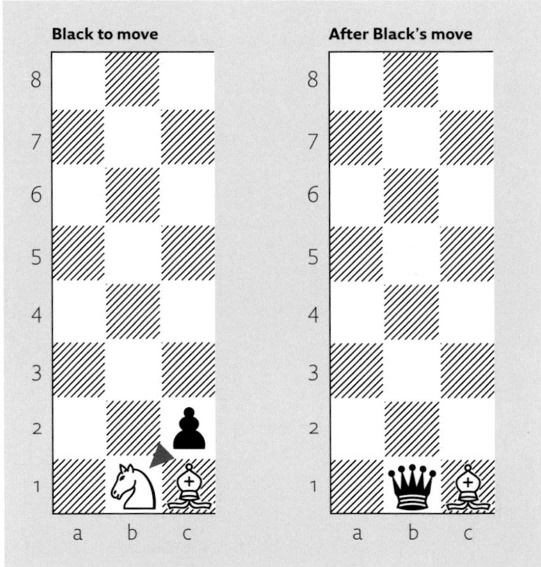

En passant – a special pawn capture

French for 'in passing', *en passant* is the name given to a particular way in which pawns can occasionally take other pawns. The opportunity to capture in this way does not happen very often, but it is important to keep the possibility in mind. For White, it happens if:

1) a white pawn is on the fifth rank;
2) a black pawn on an adjoining file advances two squares to draw level with the white pawn;
3) on the next move, the white pawn takes the black pawn as if the black pawn had only moved forward one square (the pawn takes diagonally).

If White wishes to capture *en passant*, he must do so immediately, or he loses his chance.

How this works on the board is shown below.

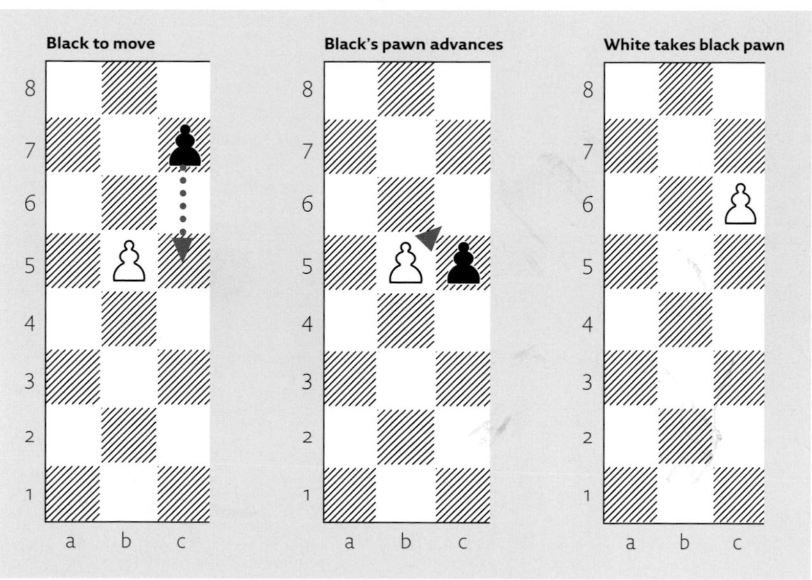

Black pawns can also take *en passant* under the same rules as for White except that black pawns have to be positioned on the fourth rank.

These three diagrams show how *en passant* works for Black.

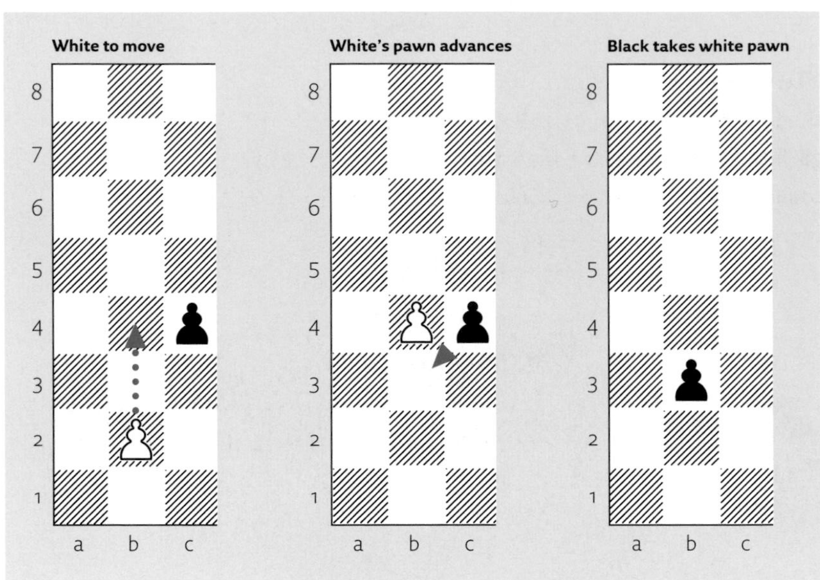

must know

It's your choice

You don't have to capture *en passant*. If the chance arises, it is your choice whether or not to capture in this way.

But remember, you can only take *en passant*:

- if your pawn is on the fifth rank for White (fourth for Black);
- if the enemy pawn on an adjoining file advances two squares;
- if you capture on the following move.

The bishop

Each side has two bishops – one on a white square and one on a black. Between them, a pair of bishops can attack every square on the chessboard but one alone can only attack half the squares.

Starting positions

White bishops start on b1 and g1; black bishops on b8 and g8. If an enemy piece stands on a black square then a white-squared bishop will never be able to threaten it and vice versa.

must know

No promotion
When a bishop moves to the far end of the board, it cannot be promoted. Only the pawn can change itself into another piece.

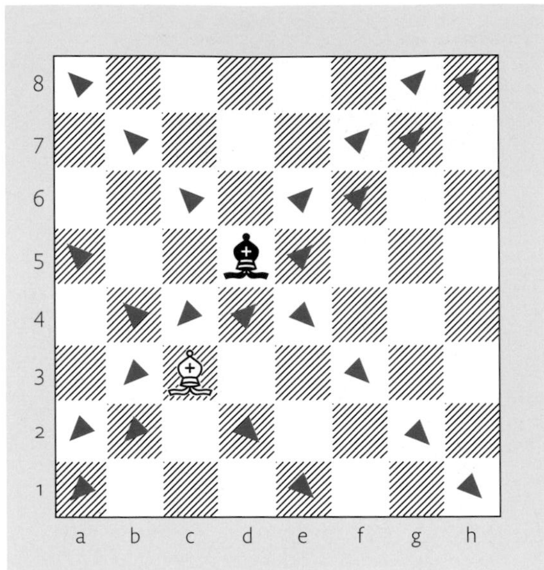

How bishops move

The bishops move along the diagonals (lines of one colour). This means that each side has one bishop that moves only on white squares and another that moves only on black squares. Bishops can move forwards or backwards to any empty square on the diagonals on which they stand, unless they are blocked, but they cannot jump over other pieces.

As you can see in the diagram above, the bishops attack many more squares than the pawns, which is why they are more powerful. The white bishop attacks (can move to) 11 squares and the black bishop attacks 13 squares. The black bishop is more powerful because it is in the centre of the board.

Bishops and knights are called minor pieces because they are worth less (see values on page 68).

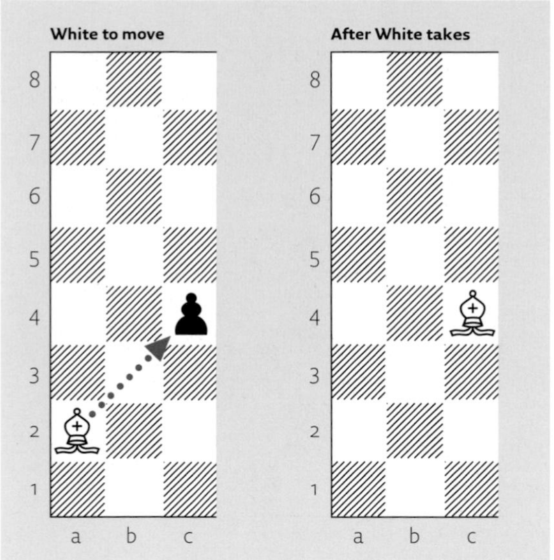

must know

Half the squares
Each side has a bishop that only moves on white squares (the white-squared bishop) and a bishop that only moves on black squares (the black-squared bishop). Each bishop can therefore only occupy, attack or defend half the squares on the board.

How bishops capture

When a bishop takes an enemy piece, it replaces the captured piece on the same square. Unlike the pawn, which moves forwards but captures diagonally, the bishop captures in the same direction that it moves.

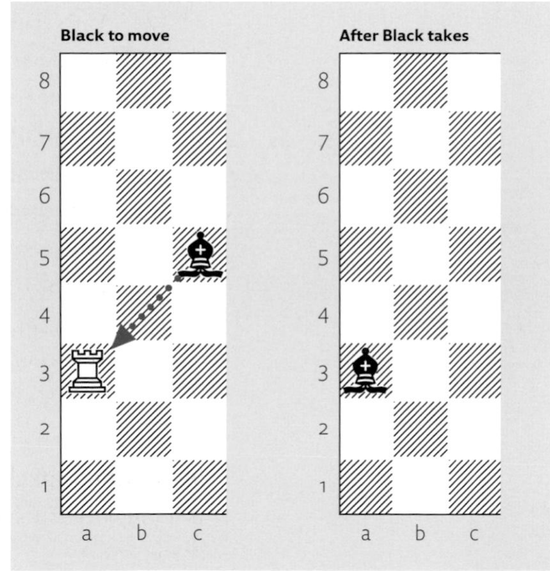

Practice with bishops

What captures and moves can the white bishop on c5 make?

The bishop can capture the a7-pawn or the bishop on f8. It can move to b6 (but would risk being taken by the a7-pawn), d6 and e7 (although both of these squares are attacked by the f8-bishop) and d4. The bishop on c5 and the pawn on b4 protect one another.

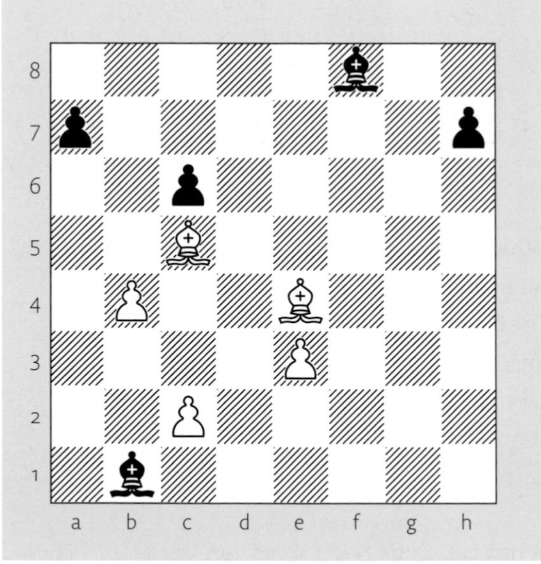

What captures and moves can the white bishop on e4 make?

The bishop can take the c6-pawn or the h7-pawn (both unprotected). It can move to d3, d5 (although it risks being taken by the c6-pawn), f3, f5, g2, g6 (risking being taken by the h7-pawn) and h1. The white pawn on c2 prevents the e4-bishop from taking the b1-bishop.

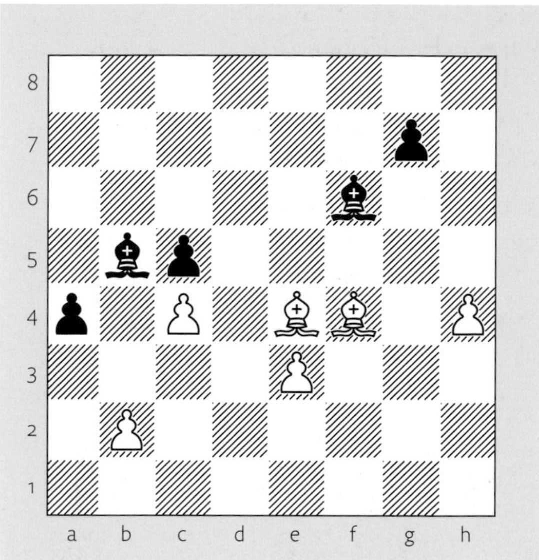

must know

Both directions
Bishops can move forwards and backwards along the diagonals. The pawn is the only chess piece that cannot move backwards.

What captures and moves can the black bishop on b5 make?

The bishop can capture the c4-pawn (which is unprotected) or move to a6, c6 (where it can be taken by the e4-bishop), d7 or e8. If this bishop stays where it is, it can be taken next move by the c4-pawn.

What captures and moves can the black bishop on f6 make?

The bishop can capture the b2-pawn or h4-pawn (both are unprotected) or move to c3 (where it can be taken by the b2-pawn), d4 (risking being taken by the e3-pawn), e5 (where it can be taken by the f4-bishop), d8, e7 and g5 (where it can be taken by the f4-bishop and the h4-pawn).

The Rook

The rook is one of the 'heavyweight' pieces of the chessboard. It is classified as a major piece and one of the key tasks for a player is to get their two rooks into action.

Starting positions

Each player has two rooks; they begin the game on the corner squares alongside the knights. White rooks start on a1 and h1; black rooks on a8 and h8.

Despite its appearance, no serious chess player ever refers to it as a 'castle'.

How rooks move

Rooks move along files and ranks, forwards, backwards or sideways (in straight lines) by as many squares as they wish, unless they are blocked. They cannot jump over other pieces.

A rook attacks as many squares as a bishop but it is the stronger piece because it can attack squares of both colours. A rook can attack any square on the board but a bishop can only attack half of them.

Your two rooks will work very well together, in both defensive and offensive play.

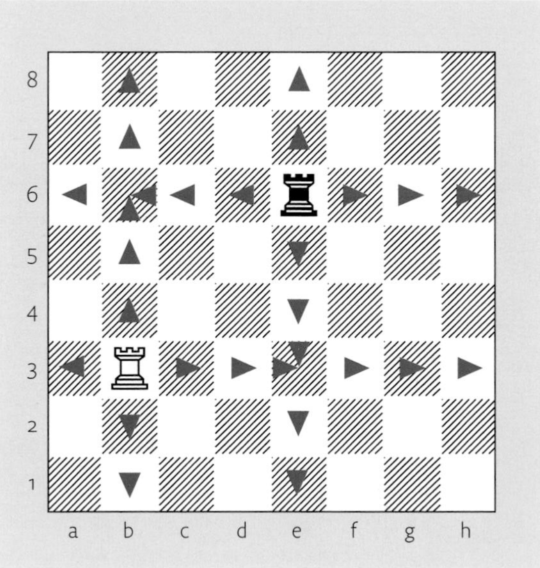

good to know

The rook's power

When placed on an open board, each rook attacks 14 squares. The problem for the rook is that it is often blocked by other pieces. As the game progresses and pieces are exchanged, rooks have more scope to move and so become more powerful.

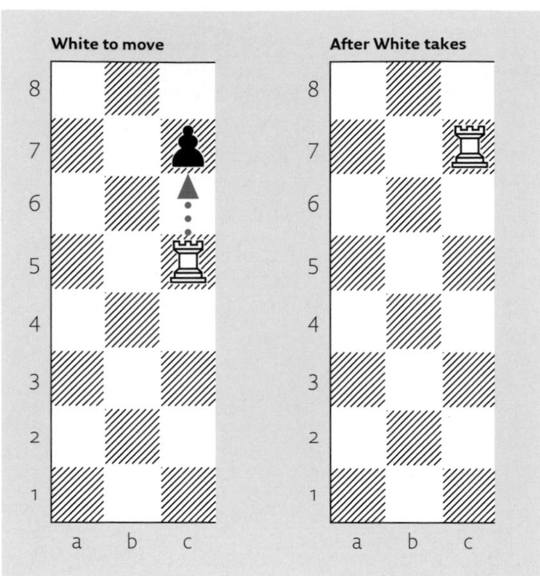

How rooks capture

When the rook takes, it replaces the captured enemy piece on the same square. The rook cannot jump over any other piece.

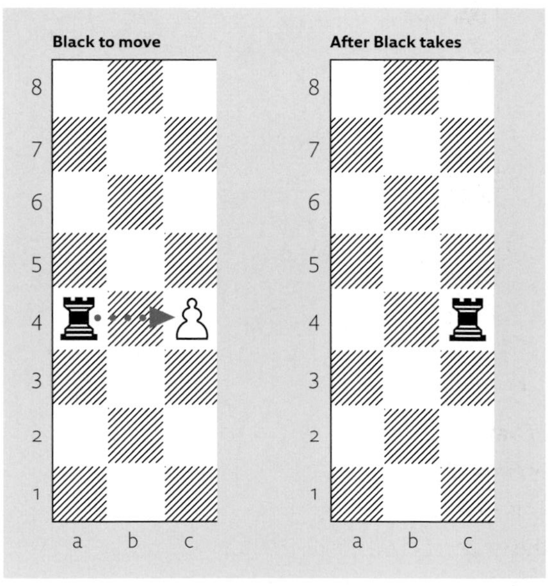

Practice with rooks

What captures and moves can the white rook on b6 make?

This rook (protected by the a5-pawn) can capture the a6-pawn (unprotected), the b7-rook (unprotected) and the g6-pawn (protected by the f7-pawn). It can move to b1, b2, b3, b4, b5 (attacked by the a6-pawn, d7-bishop and also by the b7-rook), c6 (attacked by the d7-bishop), d6, e6 (attacked by three enemy pieces) and f6.

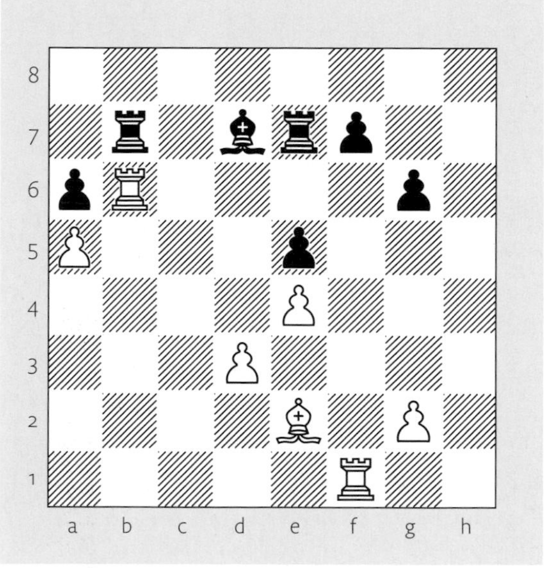

What captures and moves can the white rook on f1 make?

This rook (protected by the e2-bishop) can only take the f7-pawn (protected by the e7-rook). It can move to a1, b1, c1, d1, e1, g1, h1, f2, f3, f4 (attacked by the e5-pawn), f5 (attacked by the g6-pawn and the d7-bishop) and f6.

good to know

Protected or unprotected

Not all captures are good moves. If you take a protected piece your opponent will often recapture and you may lose out. It is usually safer to capture an unprotected piece. (See the value of the pieces on page 68.)

did you know?

Working together
Rooks work very well in pairs. When both rooks occupy the same file, a player is said to have 'doubled rooks'. Such rooks are very powerful and can easily penetrate the opponent's position.

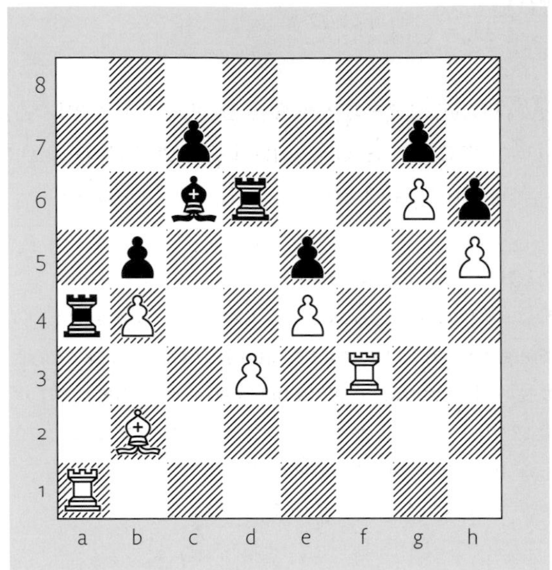

What captures and moves can the black rook on a4 make?

The rook can capture the a1-rook (protected by the b2-bishop) or the b4-pawn (unprotected). It can move to a2, a3, a5 (which is attacked by the b4-pawn), a6, a7 and a8, but on all of these squares it can be taken by the a1-rook. On a4 this black rook is protected by the b5-pawn and on a8 it would be protected by the c6-bishop.

What captures and moves can the black rook on d6 make?

This rook can capture the d3-pawn (protected by the f3-rook) or the g6-pawn (protected by the h5-pawn). It can move to d4 (attacked by the b2-bishop), d5 (attacked by the e4-pawn), d7, d8, e6 and f6 (attacked by the f3-rook but protected by the g7-pawn). On d6 the c7-pawn protects it and it is not attacked by White.

The queen

Wherever the queen is placed, it will have a tremendous influence. It is the most powerful piece on the chessboard and, along with the rook, is the other 'major' piece.

Starting positions

Each side has one queen. The white queen begins the game on d1 (a white square) and the black queen begins the game on d8 (a black square). This means that the queens begin the game facing one another (but with two pawns between them) and on a square of the same colour as themselves.

must know

Queen's file
The d-file is also known as the queen's file, because that's the file where the two queens begin the game.

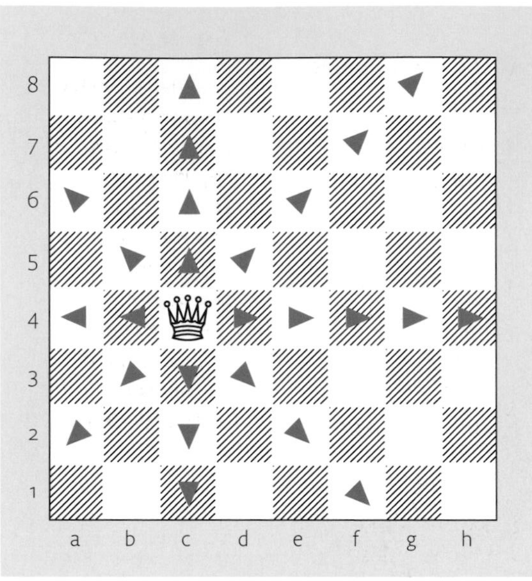

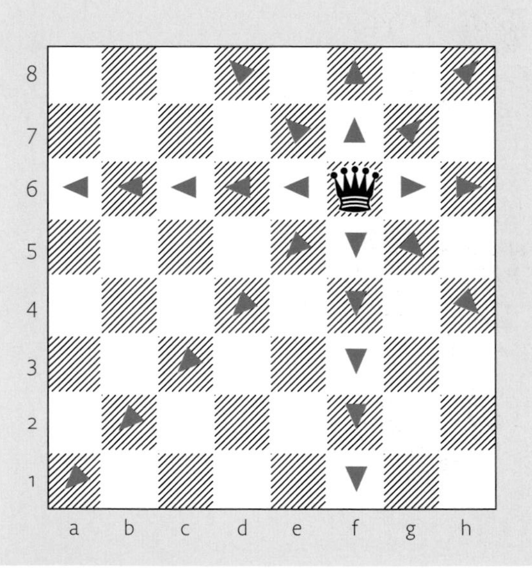

How the queen moves

The queen moves in the same way as a rook and a bishop put together, forwards, backwards, sideways or along a diagonal – any number of squares.

While the queen cannot jump over any other piece, it is the strongest piece because it can attack more squares than any other.

Because the queen is the most powerful piece on the board, it is also the most valuable. Consequently, when it is attacked, it will usually have to retreat – it is too important to lose!

How the queen captures

In these three examples both the white and black queens can take any of the other pieces shown. The queen captures in the same way as a bishop or a rook, by replacing the captured enemy piece on its square.

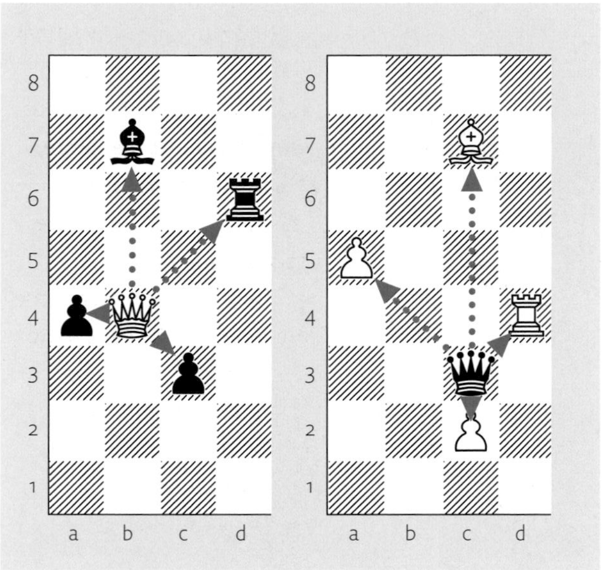

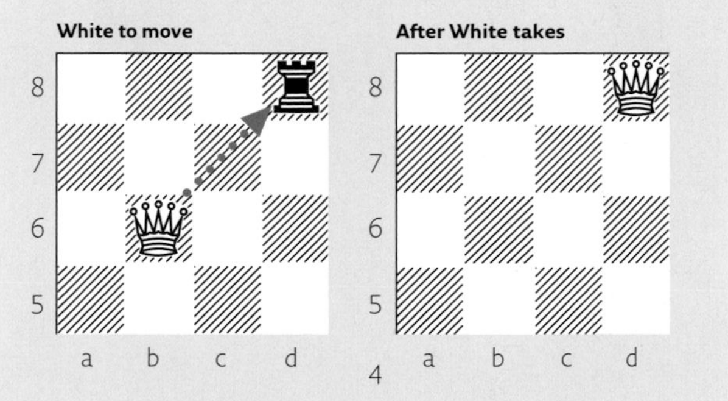

did you know?

A powerful leader
The queen attacks more squares than any other piece. A queen can attack between 21 and 27 squares at once, depending on whether it stands on a corner square or closer to the centre of the board.

good to know

Queen power

Like the rook, the queen is often blocked by other pieces and its power reduced. In theory, the more squares a piece can reach, the easier it is to block. A queen near the centre could move to a maximum of 27 squares but there are almost bound to be other pieces, of either colour, standing in the way. The queen doesn't get blocked like a rook, it just gets blocked. However, the longer the game goes on and pieces are exchanged, the more the power of the queen grows.

Practice with the queen

What captures and moves can the white queen make?

The queen can capture the a5-pawn (which is protected by the a8-rook), the a8-rook (which is protected by the d8-rook), the d6-pawn (protected by both the d8-rook and f8-bishop), the f5-pawn (protected by the g6-pawn) and the f7-pawn (which is unprotected).

The queen can move to b5, b7, c4, c5 (which is attacked by the d6-pawn), c6, d1, d2, d3, d4, e4 (which can be attacked by the f5-pawn), e5 (which is attacked by the d6-pawn), e6 (which is attacked by the f7-pawn) and f3.

Positioned on d5, the queen is not protected but neither is it be attacked.

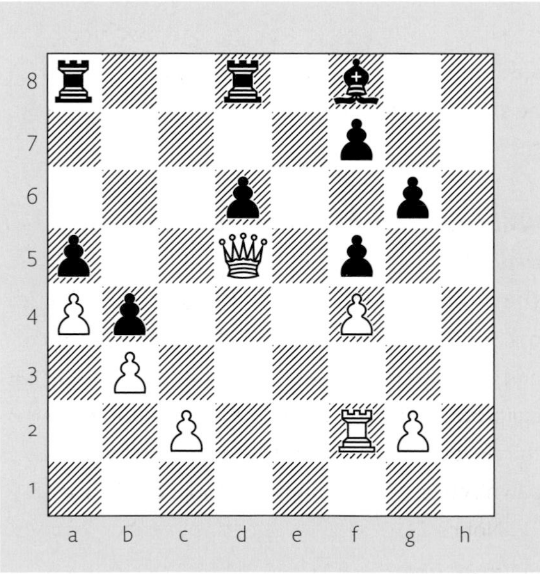

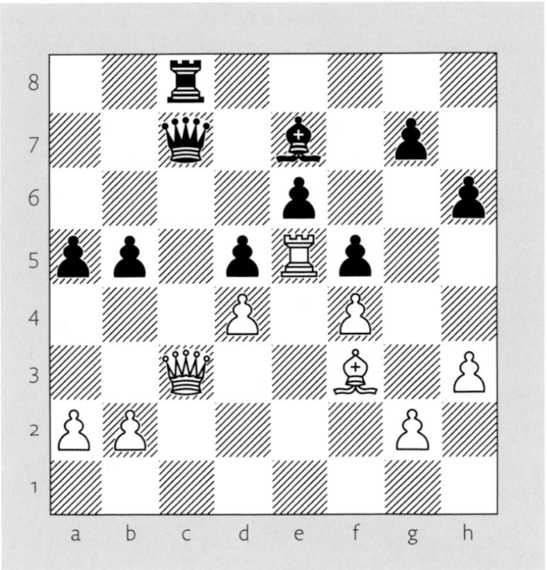

This chessboard is more crowded than the one opposite. There are more pieces and they block some of the queen's moves. The black queen could be taken by the white queen, but the c8-rook could then recapture.

What captures and moves can the black queen make?

The black queen can capture the c3-queen (protected by the b2-pawn) or the e5-rook (protected by the d4- and f4-pawns). The queen can move to a7, b6, b7, b8, c4 (protected by the b5- and d5-pawns, as well as by the c8-rook), c5 (attacked by the c3-queen and the d4-pawn), c6 (protected by the c8-rook), d6, d7 and d8.

Notice that the black queen is the only defender of the a5-pawn, which is attacked by the white queen. It is also the only defender of the c8-rook and e7-bishop (which are not under immediate threat).

The knight

The knight is the chess piece most commonly used to represent the game of chess in photographs and advertisements because it is the most distinctive-looking chess piece.

Starting positions

Each side has two knights that begin the game standing next to the rooks. White knights start on b1 and g1; black knights on b8 and g8. The knight has an unusual way of moving around the board.

How knights move

The move of the knight consists of two parts – one square along a file or rank, forwards, backwards or sideways, and then one square diagonally. If there is a piece in the way, white or black, the knight jumps over it without capturing it.

A knight is roughly the same value as a bishop but it is a very different piece. It can reach any square on the board but it is a short-range piece and so will take several moves to cross the board.

The closer a knight is to the centre of the board, the more squares it attacks and that makes it much more powerful.

The knight, like the bishop, is a minor piece.

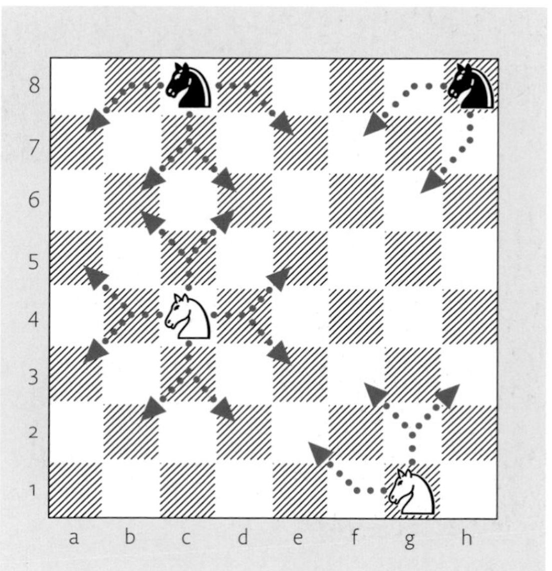

did you know?

Moving backwards

For some reason that no-one can explain satisfactorily, it is more difficult to foresee a backwards knight move.

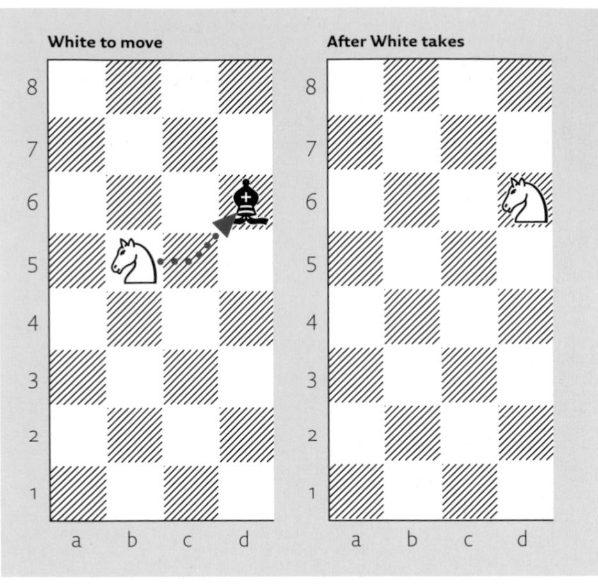

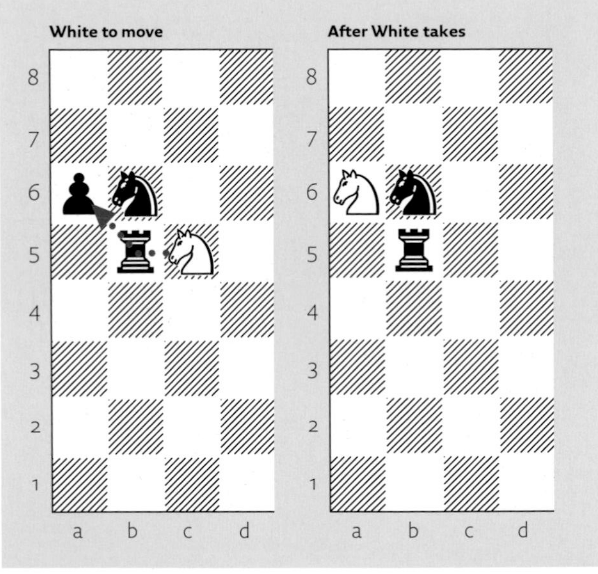

How knights capture

A knight only captures when it lands on the same square as an enemy piece. It jumps over pieces in between without affecting them.

The knight's move is so unusual that it takes a little getting used to, which is why there are some examples over the next few pages. You should use a board and set and work through them carefully, to try to get used to this singular chess piece.

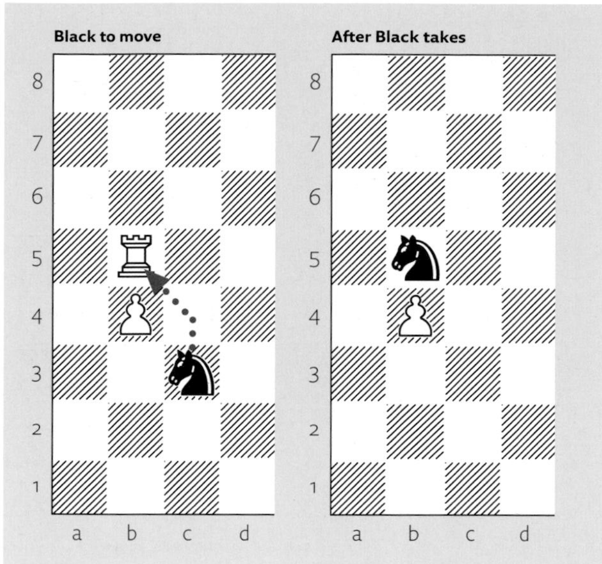

did you know?

Change of colour
When a knight moves, it always ends up on a square of a different colour from the one it started on.

Because it can jump over any other piece, the knight cannot be blocked. This makes it especially useful in crowded positions where it can often pick its way between the two armies.

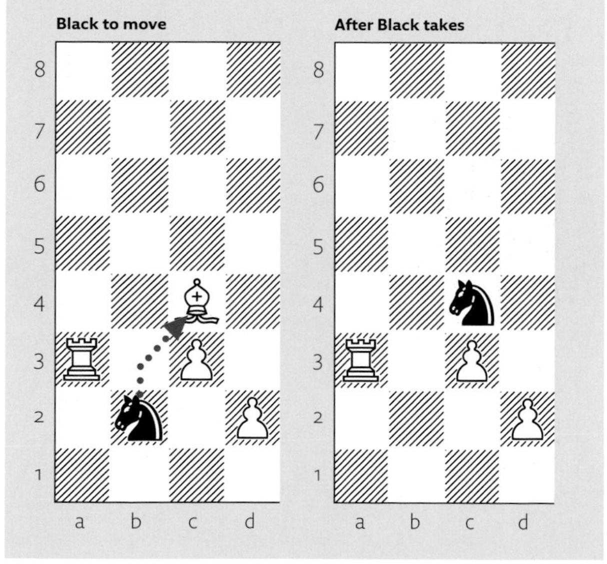

Practice with knights

What are the quickest ways for the white knight on b2 to take the g6-pawn?

There are three ways of doing it in three moves:
1) d3, e5, g6; **2)** d3, f4, g6; **3)** c4, e5, g6

What are the quickest ways for the white knight on b6 to take the g6-pawn?

There are six ways of doing it in three moves:
1) c4, e5, g6; **2)** c8, e7, g6; **3)** d5, f4, g6; **4)** d5, e7, g6; **5)** d7, e5, g6; **6)** d7, f8, g6

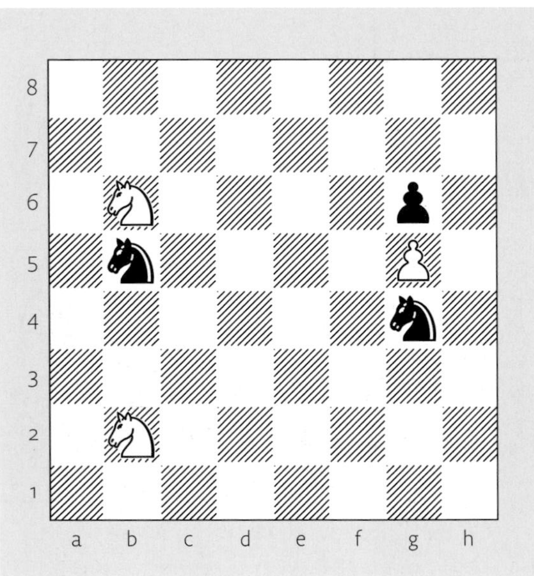

What are the quickest ways for the black knight on b5 to take the g5-pawn?

There are six ways of doing it in three moves:
1) c3, e4, g5; **2)** c7, e6, g5; **3)** d4, e6, g5; **4)** d4, f3, g5; **5)** d6, e4, g5; **6)** d6, f7, g5

What are the quickest ways for the black knight on g4 to take the g5-pawn?

There are five ways of doing it in three moves:
1) e5, f3, g5; **2)** e5, f7, g5; **3)** f2, e4, g5; **4)** f2, h3, g5; **5)** h2, f3, g5. If you begin with f6 or h6, then the pawn can take the knight!

What captures and moves can the white knight on c3 make?

The knight can capture the b5-pawn (defended by the a6-pawn). It can move to a4 (which is attacked by the b5-pawn), a2, b1, d1, d5, e2 and e4.

What captures and moves can the white knight on f5 make?

The knight can capture the d6-pawn or the g7-pawn (both are undefended). It can move to d4 (which is attacked by both black knights), e3, e7 (which is attacked by the c6-knight), g3 and h6 (which is attacked by the g7-pawn).

What captures and moves can the black knight on c6 make?

The knight can capture the a5-pawn (which is undefended). It can move to a7, b4, b8, d4 (which is attacked by the f5-knight and is defended by the f3-knight), d8, e5 and e7 (which is attacked by the f5-knight).

What captures and moves can the black knight on f3 make?

The knight can capture the d2-pawn (which is undefended), the g5-pawn (defended by the h4-pawn) or the h4-pawn (defended by the f5-knight). The f3-knight can move to d4 (which is attacked by the f5-knight but is defended by the c6-knight), e1, e5, g1 and h2.

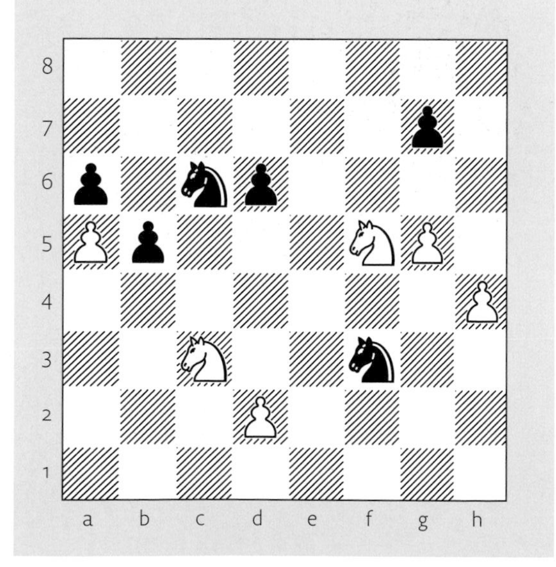

must know

Tricky knights

It takes practice to get used to the knight's move. However, it's important to be completely at ease with it and its oddities. Try inventing some exercises of your own similar to those on page 44.

The king

Not only is the king the most important and the tallest piece on the chessboard, but also the weakest! Interestingly, the entire game of chess is centred around the weakest piece.

Starting positions

Each side has one king and they begin the game standing opposite one another on e1 and e8. The e-file is also called the king's file for this reason.

How the king moves

The king can only move one square in any direction, backwards, forwards, sideways or diagonally, but it can never move on to a square where it is attacked. In addition, the king cannot move on to a square that is next to the other king.

In the diagram, the black king can move to any of the eight squares which surround it. However, the white king only has seven possible moves. It is not allowed to move to d4 because that square is attacked by the black pawn on c5.

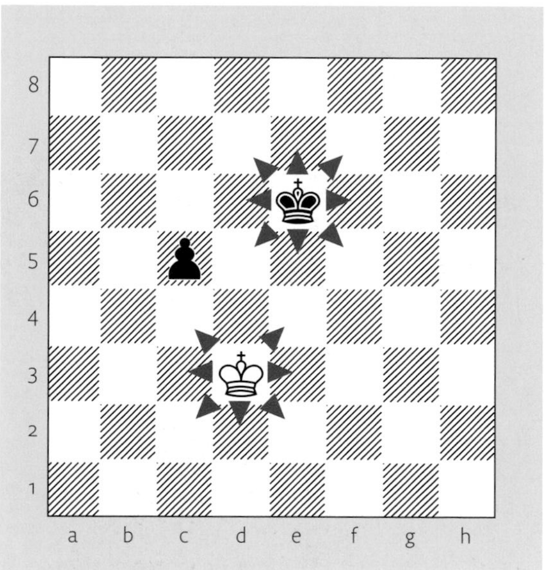

must know

Preserve your king

You must always look after your king! This is the most important rule of chess. So much so, that a king is never allowed to move to an attacked square and **must** be rescued immediately if it is threatened by your opponent.

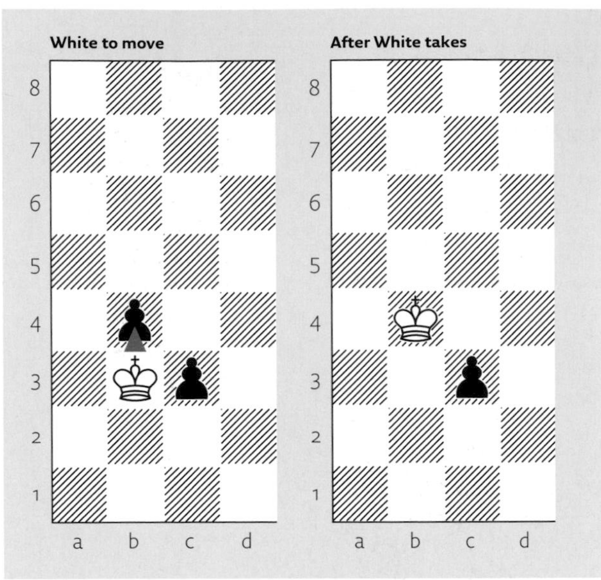

How the king captures

The white king cannot take the c3-pawn because it is defended by the b4-pawn (see **must know** opposite). The king can take the b4-pawn.

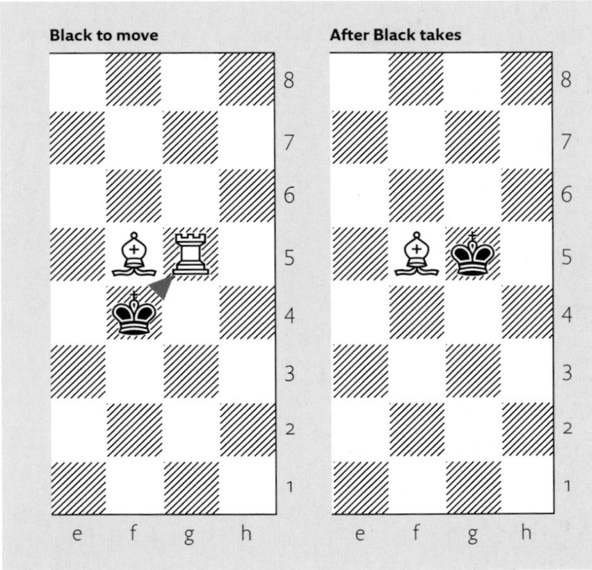

The black king cannot take the bishop because it is defended by the rook. The king can take the undefended rook.

Practice with the king

What captures and moves can the white king make?

The white king can take the b4-pawn but not the d4-pawn (which is defended by the bishop and by the rook). The king can move to b5 or d3. It cannot move to c3 (where it is attacked by both black pawns); c5 (where it is attacked by the bishop) or d5 (where it is attacked by the black rook).

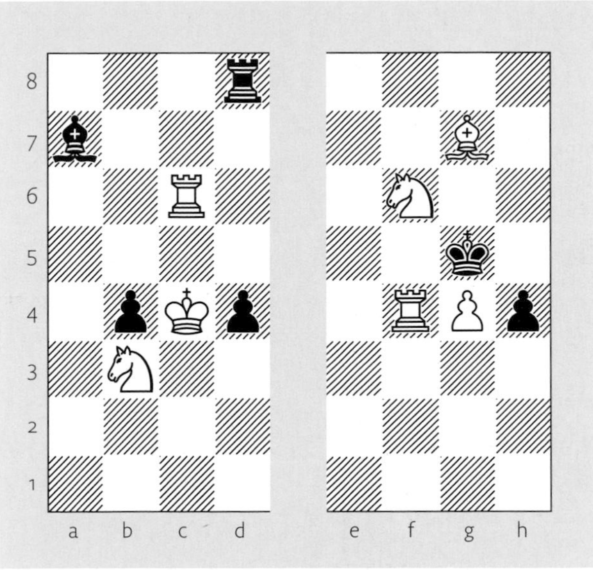

What captures and moves can the black king make?

The black king can take the rook but not the pawn (which is defended by the rook and by the knight) or the knight (which is defended by the rook and by the bishop). The black king can only move to g6. It cannot move to f5 (which is attacked by both rook and pawn), h5 (where it is attacked by the pawn and knight) or h6 (where it is attacked by the bishop).

must know

Forbidden!
Because a king cannot move to a square where it is attacked, it can never take a defended piece because the defender would then be attacking the king.

must know

Game over
The king is the weakest piece because it is the head of the army. If it is captured, the battle is over.

What captures and moves can the white king make?
The white king can take the black knight and nothing else. The white king can only move to b1. The black queen attacks a1, a2, a3, b3 and c2. The black knight attacks both a2 and b3, while the black pawn stops the king moving to either a3 or c3.

What captures and moves can the black king make?
The black king has no captures and only one move: to h5. The white rooks defend one another and the pawn defends the bishop. f5 and f6 are attacked by both rooks (and f6 by the bishop as well). The f7-rook is attacking g7 and h7. The bishop is attacking h6.

Check

A check is any move that attacks a king. It is such an important move that it has its own name. A check cannot be ignored. The attacked king must get out of check immediately!

Chess etiquette

If you play a move that attacks the enemy king (threatens to capture it), it is polite to warn your opponent by saying 'check' (quietly).

must know

King rule

Remember, the king cannot take a defended piece because that would mean moving into check.

What white moves put the black king in check?

The queen can move to b1 or b3; the rook can move to d7; the bishop can move to c6; and the pawn can move to c6. The knight cannot put the king in check.

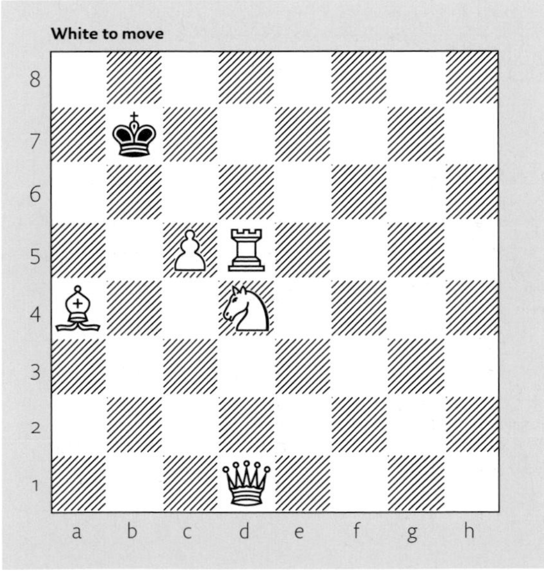

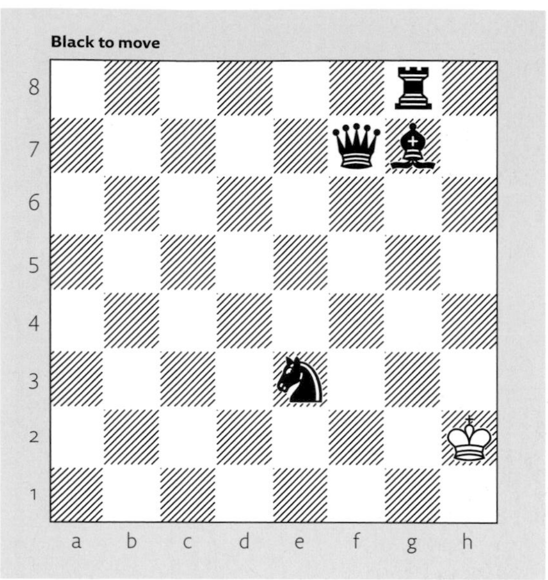

What black moves put the white king in check?

The queen can move to f2, f4 or h5; the rook can move to h8; the bishop can move to e5; and the knight can move to f1 or g4.

What white moves put the black king in check?

The queen can capture the a5-pawn (the queen will be protected by the bishop) or move to b6, b7, b8, c5 (the queen will be unprotected on c5 and the black king could take it) or d4; the rook can move to b1; the bishop can capture the a5-pawn (the bishop will be protected by the queen) or can move to d6; the knight can move to d3; and the pawn can move to a3.

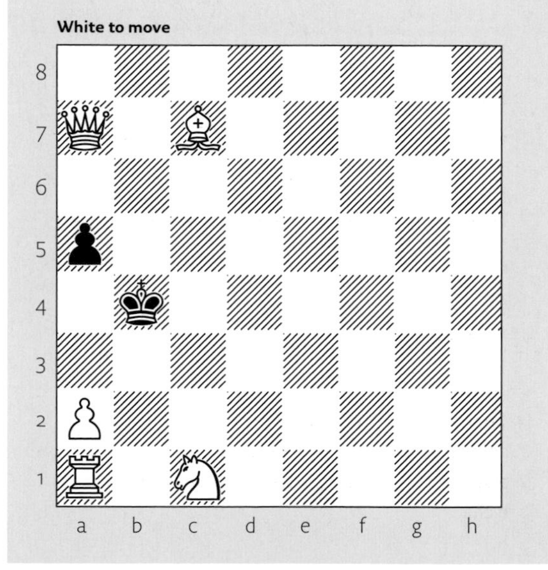

What black moves put the white king in check?

The queen can capture the f3-pawn (but the white king could then take the queen) or take the rook on g6; the black rook can move to g4 (but both the f3-pawn and the g6-rook could then take the black rook) or h2 (but the white king could take the rook); the bishop can move to h3; and the knight can check from f4.

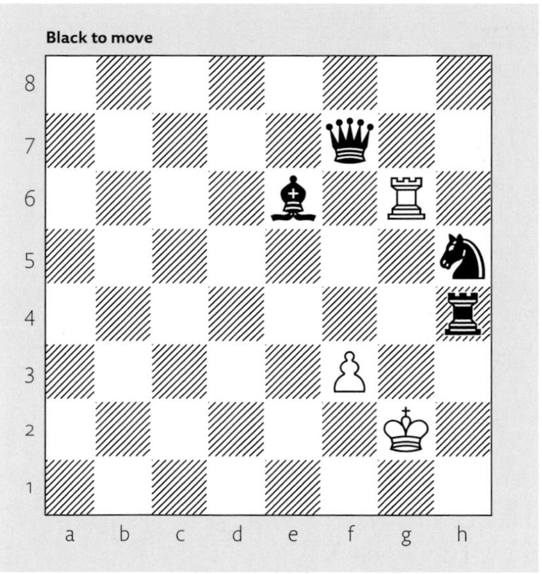

must know

Get out of check

Not only should a king not move into check, it **must** get out of check, immediately! In addition, you are not allowed to play **any** move, with any piece, that puts your king into check.

More about check

When a king is checked, it must get out of check on its next move. There are no exceptions and there can be no delay.

There are three possible ways out of check: take the piece giving check, move the king to a square that is not under attack, or block the check with another piece by putting it in between the checking piece and the king (but you cannot block a check from a knight, because the knight can jump over any blocker).

What white moves get the king out of check?

The queen can take the rook on a5; the king can move to b4, c4 or d6 (all four other king moves would leave the king in check, which is not allowed); the bishop can move to b5, which would block the check.

must know

No choice

Don't forget, you are not allowed to make any move, with any piece, that will put your king into check. If your opponent attacks your king, you must get out of check immediately.

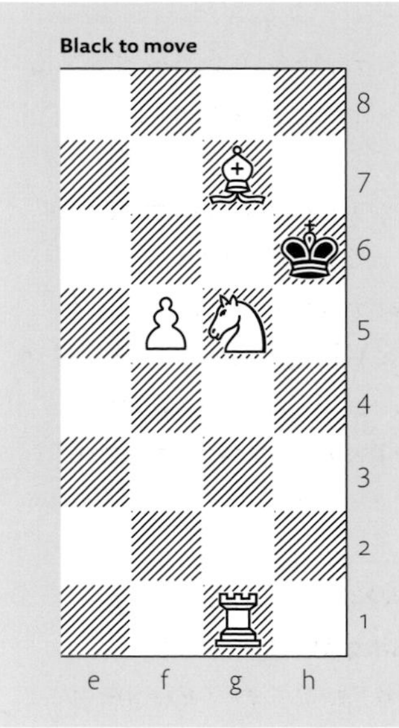

What black moves get the king out of check?

The king can take the bishop on g7 or it can move to h5. The king cannot move to g6 as it would be in check from the f5-pawn; the king cannot take the knight on g5 because it would be in check from the rook on g1. The king cannot move to h7 as it would then be in check from the knight. There are no ways of blocking the check.

What white moves do not place the king in check?

The king on b1 can only move to a1 (which leaves the c1-rook unprotected). The king cannot go to c2 because it would be in check from the d2-rook. The b2-pawn cannot take the a3-pawn as that would leave the white king in check from the black queen. The b2-pawn may, however, move to b3 or b4 (but it will be unprotected on b4). The c1- (white) rook cannot move along the c-file as that would leave the white king in check from the d1- (black) rook, but the c1-rook is allowed to take the d1-rook (even though it could then be taken by the d2- [black] rook).

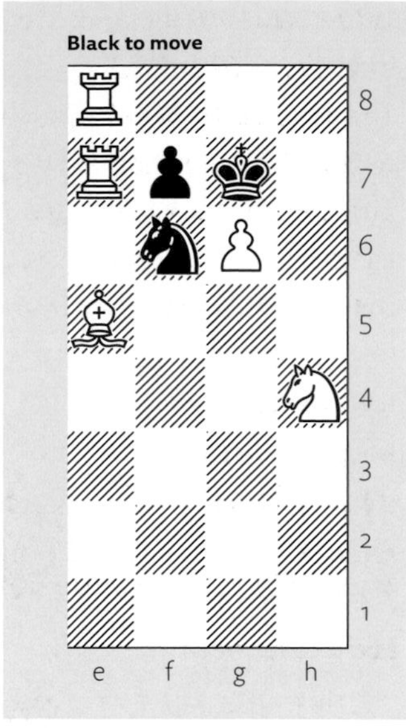

What black moves do not place the king in check?

The f7-pawn cannot take the g6-pawn as that would leave the black king in check from the e7-rook. The f6-knight is not allowed to move as that would leave the black king in check from the bishop. The black king cannot move to f8, g8 or h8 as that would leave it in check from the e8-rook. Neither may the king move to h7 (because it would be in check from the g6-pawn) or take the g6-pawn (which would leave it in check from the knight). The only king move and, in fact, Black's only possible move in this position, is to h6.

What black moves put the white king in check?

The knight can put the king in check by moving to a6 or d3. The rook can check by moving to a4 (protected by the knight) or b8.

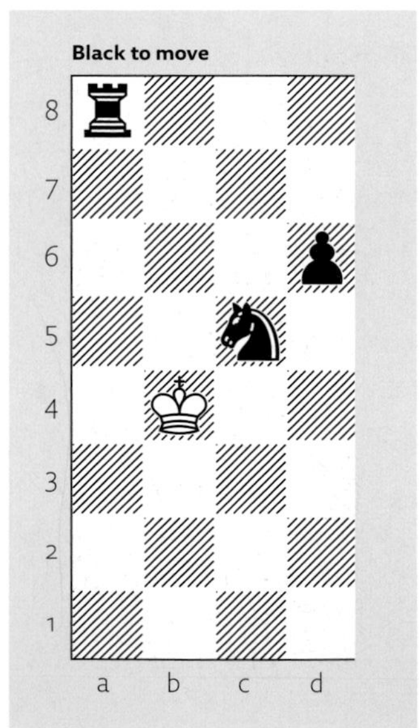

What white moves put the black king in check?

The knight can check by moving to f4 or f8. The bishop can check by moving to e4 and the pawn can check by moving to h5 (but the king could then capture it).

What black moves put the white king in check?

The knight can take the a2-pawn or move to d3. The rook can move to c8.

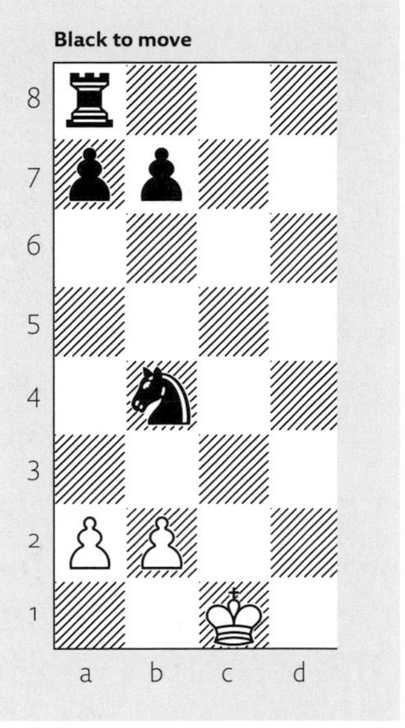

What white moves put the black king in check?

The rook can move to f3 or g1. The queen can move to f2, f3, f4, g4 (but is undefended here, which means the king could take it), g5 (here, the f6-pawn could take it), g6 and h3 (but again it will be undefended).

Discovered check

When a piece moves and doesn't give check itself, but opens up a check from another piece standing behind it, this is known as a discovered check.

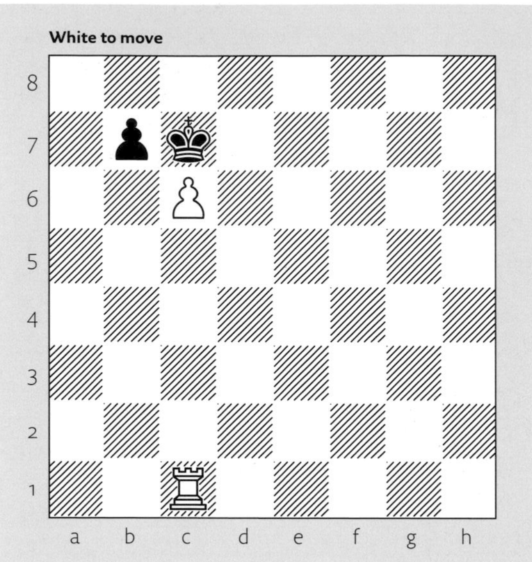

What white move reveals a discovered check?

The white rook is on the same file as the black king, which means that when the c6-pawn takes the b7-pawn the king is in check! The pawn doesn't give check, but the rook does. Black must get out of check next move.

What black move reveals a discovered check?

Any move by the black knight on f3 will leave the white king in check from the black bishop. The knight doesn't give check, but the bishop does. White must get out of check next move.

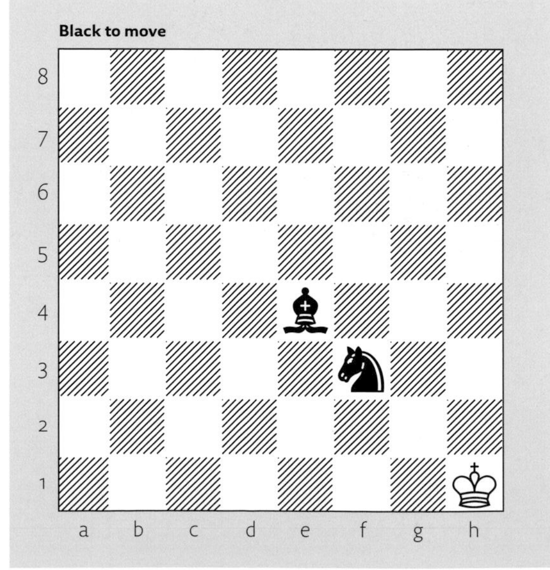

Double check

In a discovered check, if the piece that moves also gives check, then the king will find itself in check from two pieces.

What white move puts the black king in double check?

Any move by the white bishop will mean that the king is in check from the queen, but if the bishop moves to d4, then it will also be in check from the bishop – double check!

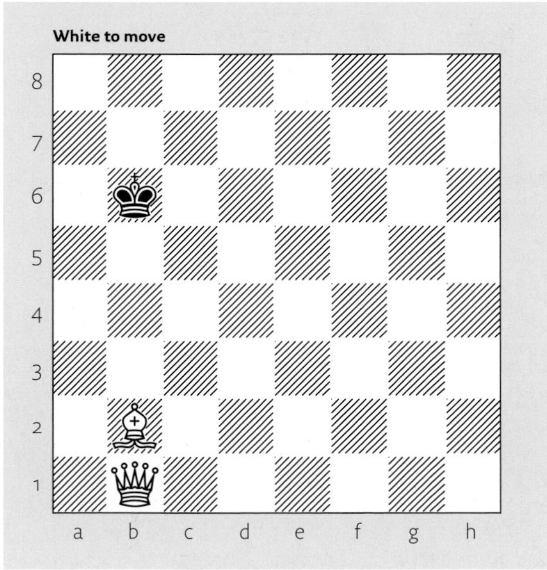

must know

Eyes open

It is quite common for beginners to have an illegal position on the board because they have not noticed a discovered or a double check. Always keep your eyes open for possible checks.

good to know

Powerful moves

Double checks are very powerful because the attacked king must get out of both checks on the next move. The only way to do this is with a king move. The other two ways out of check, taking the checking piece or blocking the check, are not possible when there are two checks. But taking one checking piece is possible if that also gets the king out of the other check, as in the example on the right.

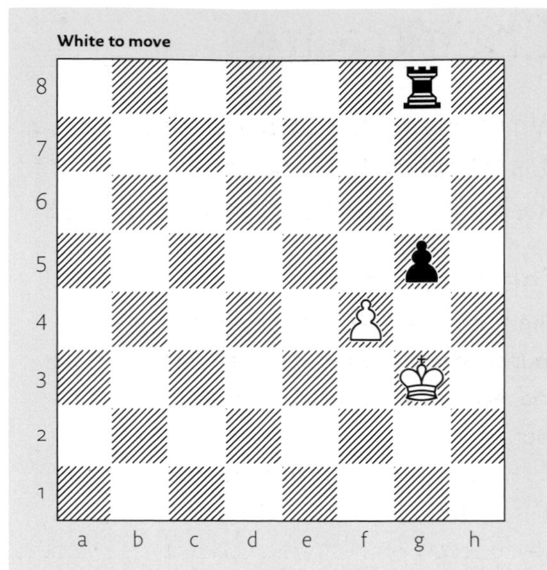

What black move puts the white king in double check?

If the g5-pawn captures the f4-pawn it leaves the king in check from both rook and pawn – double check!

The only way out of a double check is to move the king, sometimes taking one of the checking pieces. For instance, in the above example, after Black plays g5-pawn takes f4-pawn (double check), White could reply with king takes Black's new f4-pawn, getting out of both checks.

Checkmate

When a king gets into a position where it cannot avoid capture, it is 'checkmated' and that is the end of the game. That's why the king is the weakest piece. It must be protected at all times.

The aim in chess

The object of a game of chess is not to take all of your opponent's pieces, it is to attack his or her king and reach a position in which the king cannot avoid capture.

Here are some checkmate positions. In all of these positions, a king is in check and there is no way to get out of check. It is checkmate, the battle is over and it is the end of the game.

Work out which enemy piece is attacking the king (giving check) and why all of the moves available to the king will leave it in check.

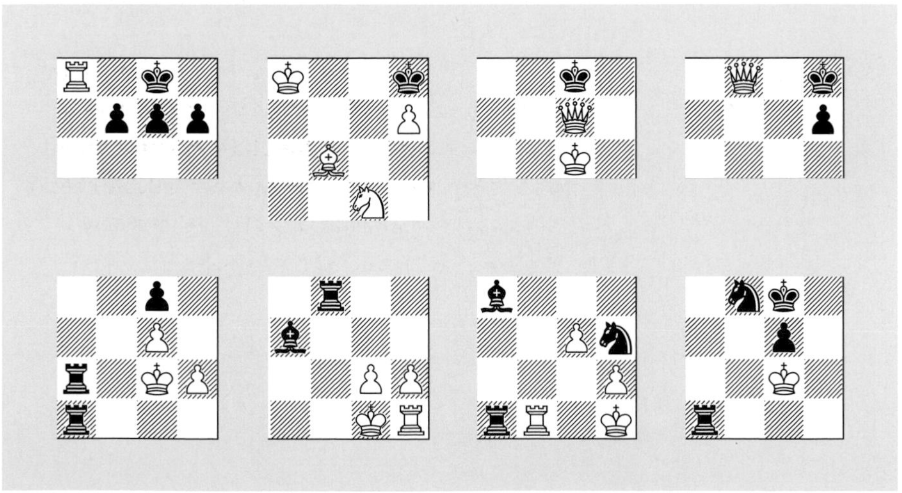

Try to checkmate

Which white move gives checkmate in each position? Try each of the checks until you find one that Black cannot get out of.

In the left-hand diagram, all of the queen checks allow the black king to move, but if the bishop moves to d6 it is checkmate.

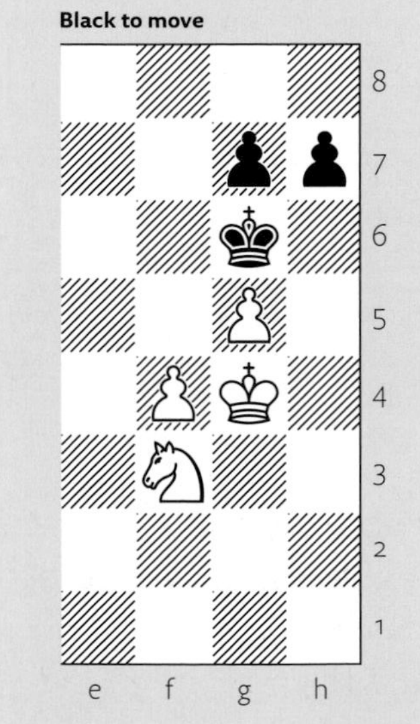

In the right-hand diagram, the pawn check from f5 and the knight check from h4 can both be answered by the black king moving to f7, but if the knight moves to e5, it is checkmate.

Stalemate

In the left-hand diagram, if White moves the queen to a6, Black has no legal move (every possible move with his king will be a check, so they are not allowed). However, it is not checkmate – it is not even check. Because Black cannot move, the game is over and because it isn't checkmate, no-one has won – it's a draw.

must know

Take care
Players must move alternately. When it is someone's turn to move and they don't have a legal move (and they aren't in check), then the game cannot continue. This is called **stalemate** and the result of the game is a draw.

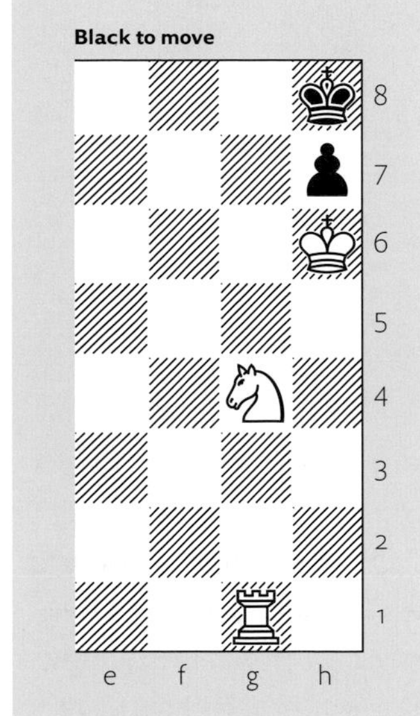

In the right-hand diagram, if White moves his knight it will be stalemate, because the white rook will prevent the black king moving to g8, and that was Black's only move.

Castling

Along with *en passant* (see pages 23–4), castling is another strange move in chess. It is a way of getting the king away from the centre of the board where it could get into danger.

Protecting the king

At the same time as protecting the king, castling is a way of getting a rook away from the corner and more into the action – all in one move!

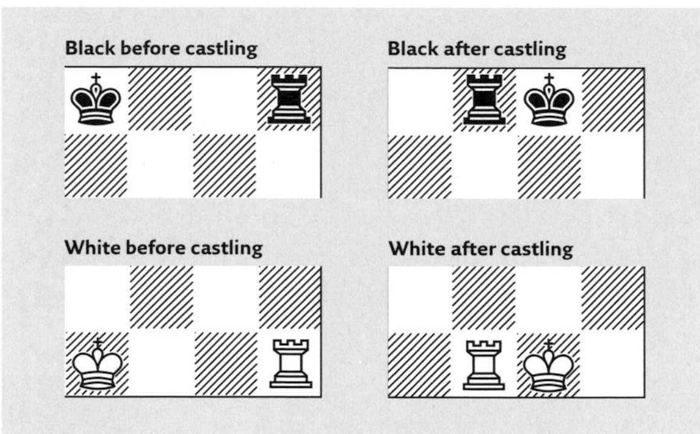

First let's look at castling on the king's side of the board (see left). The king moves two squares towards the rook and the rook jumps over the king to land next to the king – all in one move! Like the king, the rook has moved two squares.

Now castling on the queen's side. The king moves two squares towards the rook and the rook jumps over the king to land next to the king. Here, the rook moves three squares.

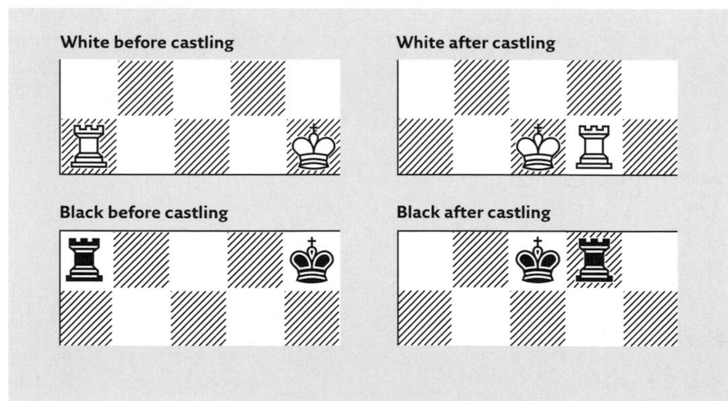

You are **not** allowed to castle if either the rook or the king has previously moved, even if they have moved back to their starting positions. In addition, castling is not allowed in the following three situations:

a) to get out of check;
b) if you end up in check;
c) if the king moves across an attacked square (if it goes 'through' check).

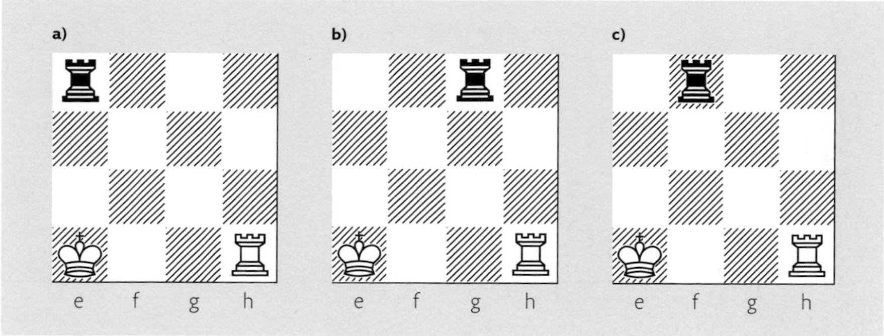

It is okay for White to castle in the following two positions as the rook is allowed to cross an attacked square and you are permitted to castle when the rook is attacked.

2 Next moves

My rook is attacked; should I move it to safety or defend it? I can take his knight, but then I will lose my piece. Is that a good exchange or a bad one? In order to answer these questions you need to know the values of the pieces and why they have those values. In chess the values of the pieces are not fixed; they vary slightly all the time according to the number of squares that each piece is attacking and also the importance of those squares. In this chapter we will help you to answer those questions.

The values of the pieces

Some pieces are more powerful than others and 'more powerful' means 'more valuable'. But just how valuable are they? The points table below gives the answer.

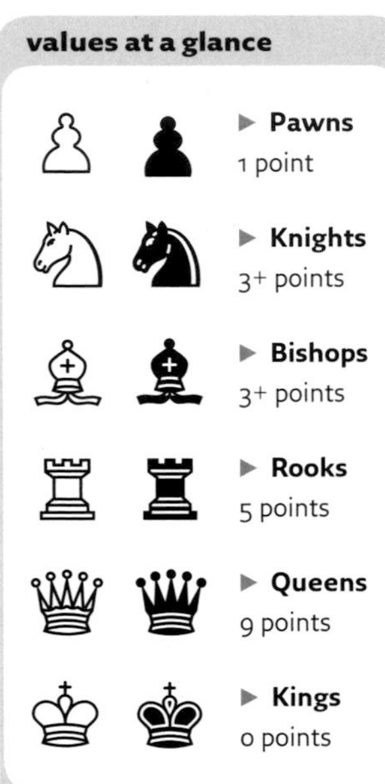

values at a glance

Piece	Value
▶ **Pawns**	1 point
▶ **Knights**	3+ points
▶ **Bishops**	3+ points
▶ **Rooks**	5 points
▶ **Queens**	9 points
▶ **Kings**	0 points

Points for pieces

The approximate values of the pieces for most of the game are shown in the table, left. The point score for each piece is given on the right-hand side.

This table illustrates that two rooks are worth more than a queen. A knight and a pawn are worth less than a rook but a knight and two pawns are worth more.

Why these values?

The values of the pieces are strongly connected to the number of squares that the pieces can attack.

The pawn

Pawns standing on the a-file and h-file only attack one square but other pawns, nearer the centre, attack two squares.

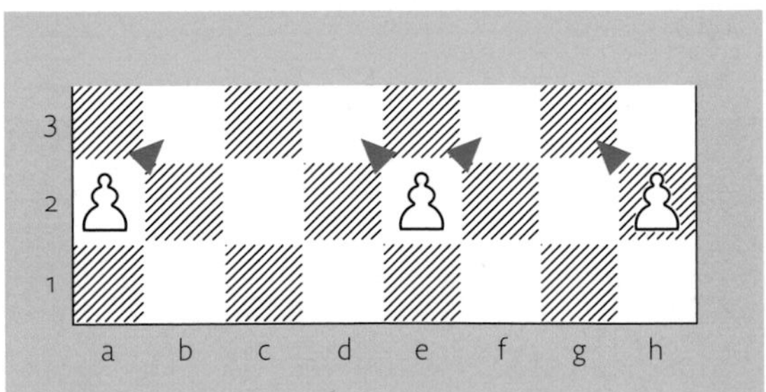

The knight

A knight positioned in the corner can only attack two squares. As the knight moves closer to the centre of the board, the number of squares it can attack increases, up to eight. The knight is a short range piece but, given time, a knight can attack any square on the board.

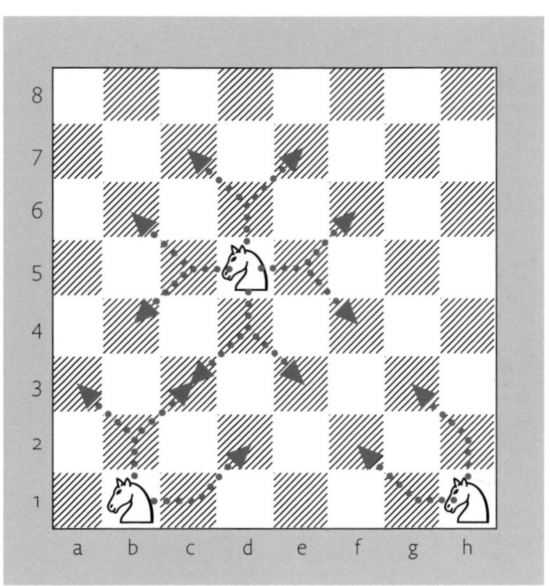

The bishop

A bishop in the corner attacks 7 squares whereas a bishop in the centre attacks 13 squares. The big drawback of the bishop is that it can only attack squares of one colour. Any enemy piece standing on a square of the other colour is perfectly safe from it.

good to know

Problems for rooks
To become effective pieces, rooks must get out of the corner of the board and into play and they are often the last piece to do this. It is usually best to move them along the back rank towards the centre files as they, ideally, need to find a file where the pawn has advanced because this will give them more scope.

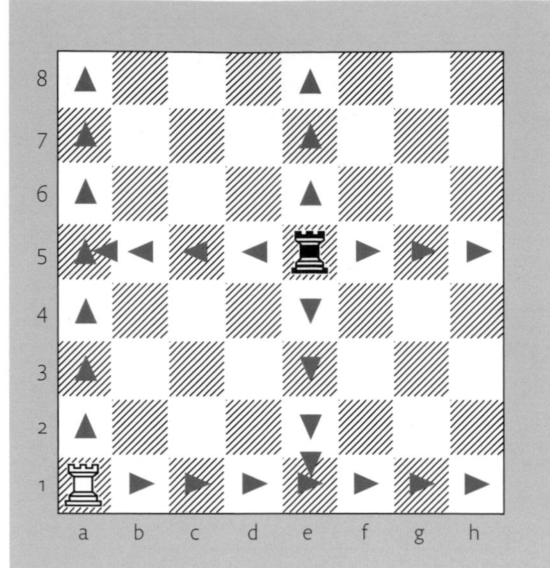

The rook

A rook attacks 14 squares no matter where it stands on (an empty) board.

The king

Usually a king has to be protected and so is worth nothing. Sometimes, when there are no longer enough pieces left to threaten checkmate, the king emerges and acts as an attacking piece. Under these circumstances the king, which can attack a maximum of eight squares, is worth about four points. The king is a good defender of other pieces.

The queen

A queen in a corner attacks 21 squares. As the queen gets closer to the centre, the number of squares it attacks increases to 27.

All pieces become stronger as they approach the centre of the board, because they can attack more squares.

Bishops, rooks and queens are long range pieces but they are often blocked by other pieces and so they are not worth quite as much as might first appear. As pieces are exchanged, those left are less likely to be blocked and so become more powerful and valuable.

Knights can only attack half as many squares as bishops. Knights cannot cover the whole board quickly but they cannot be blocked.

It generally works out that knights and bishops are worth about the same, but as the game progresses, bishops are less likely to be blocked and so may become more powerful than knights.

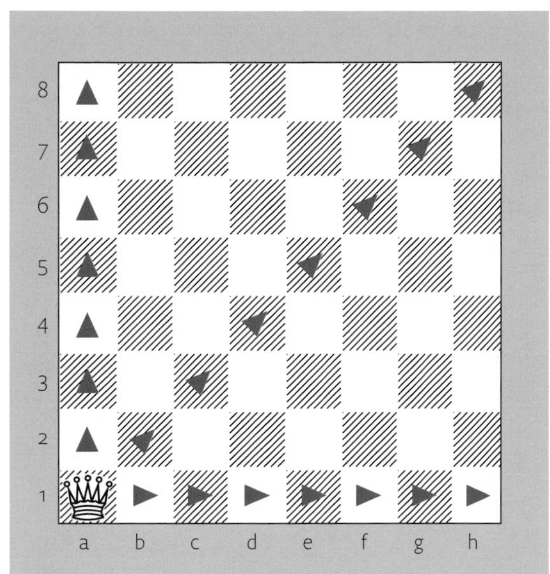

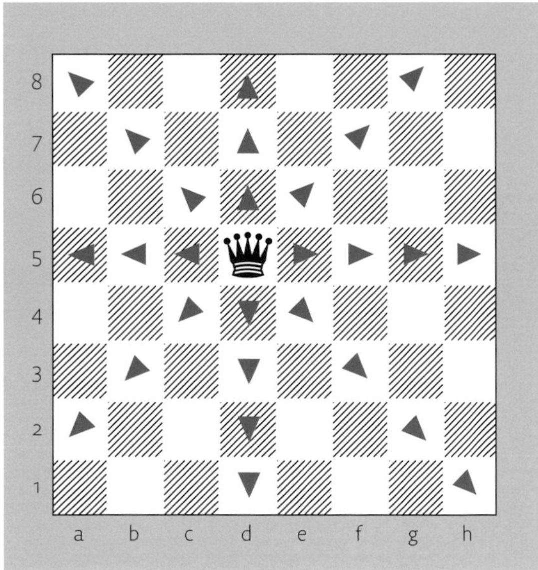

Reading and writing moves

Writing down the moves makes it possible to replay the games of the great players of the past and of today. It also makes it possible for you to write down and play over your own games.

How to write the moves

As we have seen, every square has a name. Add a capital letter to show which piece is moving and you have a move.

The initial letters are: **N** = knight (K is reserved for the king); **B** = bishop; **R** = rook; **Q** = queen; **K** = king. A move without an initial is a pawn move.

Notation

There are two ways of writing down the moves:

- the short form (which is used in this book): by giving the piece and the finishing square, for example, **Bc4**
- the long form: by giving the piece, the starting square and the finishing square, for example, **Bf1-c4.** The move number is written first, followed by White's then Black's move:
- **1 e4 e5** is a complete move (move number, white move, black move). **1...e5** is a black move ('...' shows that the white move is not given).

Key to symbols

- **-** = 'moves to' (used in the long form)
- **x** = 'captures' (**1 Nxe4** = a white knight takes whatever piece is on e4)
- **+** = 'check' (**2...Rc2+** = a black rook has moved to c2 and placed the white king in check)
- **o-o** = 'castles king's side'
- **o-o-o** = 'castles queen's side'

must know

Comments on moves

Punctuation marks are often used to give a writer's opinion of a move. The commonest marks and their meanings are:

- **?** = weak move
- **??** = blunder
- **!** = good or surprising move
- **!!** = strong and surprising move
- **!?** = interesting move
- **?!** = dubious move with some positive points

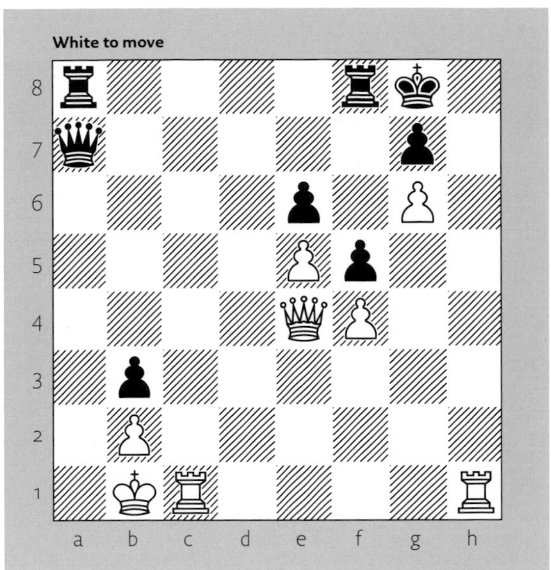

In the above diagram Black is threatening 1...Qa2 or 1...Qa1 mate, so White must act immediately:

1 Rh8+ Kxh8 (forced)

2 Qh1+ Kg8 (forced)

3 Qh7 mate! – which produces the position in the diagram on the right.

'Forced' means that the move is the only one possible. Black must get out of check!

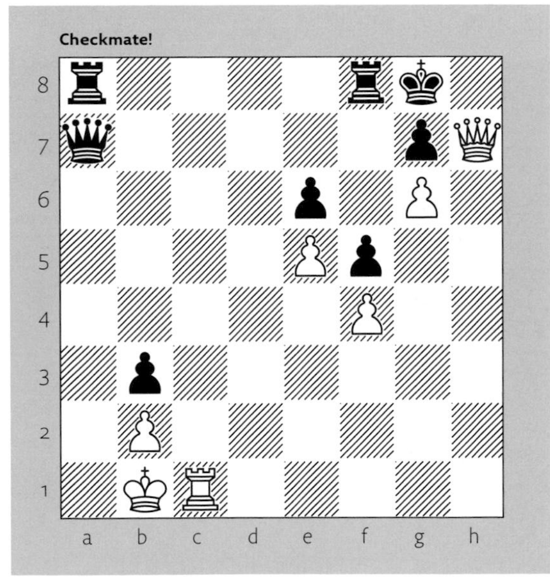

Good and bad moves

Now we know the values of the pieces, it is possible to recognise that some moves are good and some are bad. Moves that gain value are good and those that lose value are bad.

good to know

Sacrifice

A move which deliberately gives away value, in order to gain an advantage is known as a sacrifice. A 'gambit' is a sacrifice made early in the game and is explained on page 145.

Exchanges

In the example below, the capture 1 Rxf6 would be a bad move because Black could recapture either by 1...gxf6 or 1...Bxf6 and White would have lost the rook for a knight, which is known as 'the exchange'.

If 1 Bxe6, Black could recapture by 1...fxe6 or 1...Qxe6 and White would have 'exchanged' bishops with no obvious advantage to either side.

White could also play 1 Bxf6. But after the reply of 1...gxf6 or 1...Bxf6, White would have exchanged a bishop for a knight, again with no advantage.

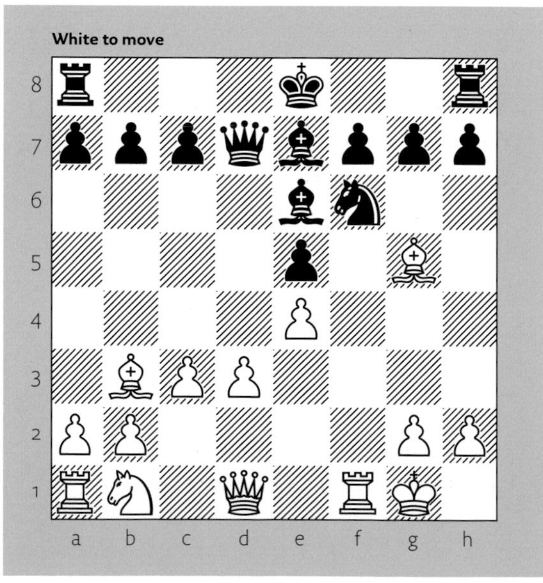

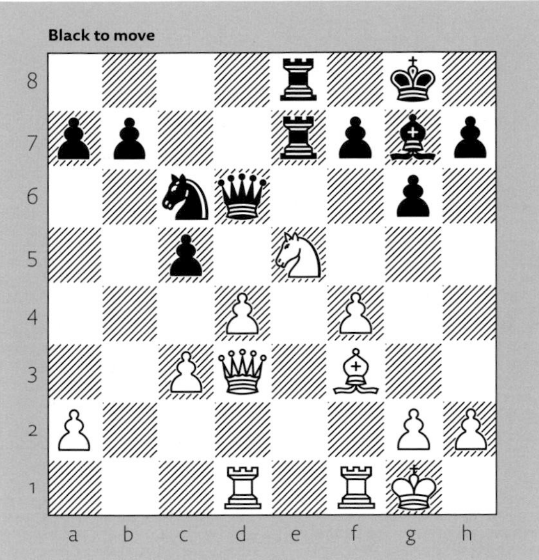

Here Black has seven possible captures – three pieces threaten the d4-pawn and four pieces can take the knight on e5.

1...cxd4 would lead to a pawn exchange after the recapture 2 cxd4. If the black knight or queen captured the d4-pawn it would lead to a loss after 2 cxd4.

If the e5-knight was captured by the e7-rook or the black queen, this would also lead to a loss after a recapture by either the d4- or f4-pawn. 1...Nxe5 and 1...Bxe5 are both possible without losing anything; they would be 'exchanges' of approximately equal value.

This position shows how useful it is to have your pieces protected by pawns – they cannot normally be taken by enemy pieces of greater value.

good to know

Exchanges or 'the exchange'

In the diagram on this page, if Black plays 1...Nxe5 and White recaptures, then they have exchanged pieces. If Black plays 1...Bxe5 and White recaptures, then they have exchanged a pair of minor pieces. If Black plays 1...Rxe5 and White recaptures, then Black has lost 'the exchange'. 'The exchange' is the difference between a rook and a knight or a rook and a bishop.

must know

Writing the moves
If both rooks (or knights) can move to the same square, then you indicate which one is moving by adding the letter of the file on which it stands. If they are both on the same file, then add the number of the rank instead. Here, 1 Rab1 is short for 1 Ra1-b1 and not, therefore, 1 Rf1-b1.

Protect or move?

When one of your pieces is under attack, you have to decide whether to protect it, or move it. In the diagram below consider those options.

What are Black's choices after 1 Rab1?

How can you defend the b7-bishop and where can it move to?

You could defend the bishop by 1...Rab8 (getting this rook into play); by 1...Rfb8? (blocking in the other rook); by 1...c6? (defending with the queen, but blocking the bishop); by 1...c5? (perhaps losing this pawn); by 1...Qc8? (putting the queen out of play); 1...Qc6; or 1...Qd5 (losing the queen!).

You could move the bishop to a6 (losing it to the c4-bishop); to c8 (where it would be out of play); or to c6, d5 or e4. The bishop could also take the knight on f3 (1...Bxf3).

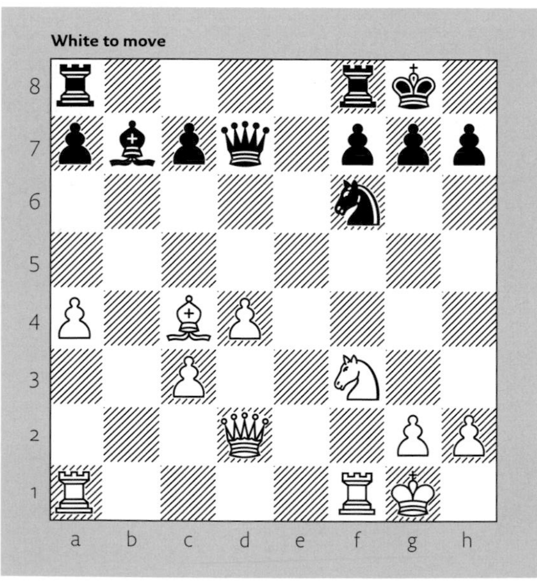

What are Black's choices after 1 Bb5?

If a piece is attacked by something of lower value then you must end the attack by taking the attacker, blocking the attack or moving the attacked piece.

If the queen captures the b5-bishop, it would be captured by the a4-pawn; c6 is possible but blocks the bishop on b7; the queen can safely move to c8, d5, d6, d8, e6, e7, f5 or g4.

Protect and recapture

If one of your pieces is being threatened, try to protect it and make a counter-attack in one move. See the diagram below and consider the various options for White.

What are White's choices after 1...Bg4?

The black bishop is threatening to take the f3-knight (the g2-pawn cannot recapture because White would then be in check from the g8 rook). White could move the f3-knight to h4 or d4 or protect it by Re3, Qd3, Qe2 or Qe3 (the last two moves attack the e7-knight as well).

What are White's choices after 1...Qb6?

How can White defend the b2-pawn?

White can move the pawn to b3 or b4 or protect it by Na4 (which also threatens the queen), Rb1 (but this takes the rook out of play) or Qc1.

If Black tries 1...d4, trying to force the c3-knight to move, White can reply 2 Nxd4 but that is risky, putting the knight between the black rook and the white queen. Moving the c3-knight is simpler – 2 Ne4 attacking the undefended f6-pawn looks good.

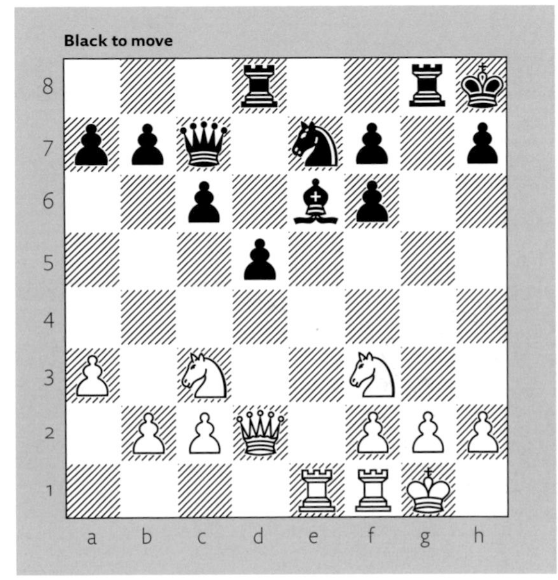

good to know

Pieces matter

You need to keep your pieces protected so that you can recapture when your opponent takes one of your pieces. While you are learning, it may not matter too much if you fall behind in the piece count, but later, falling behind means losing the game.

watch out!

Mind your king
A check, or a possible check, is always an important consideration. So, when you are calculating captures, always remember to keep an eye open for an exposed king.

Protected enough?

Sometimes a piece can be under attack and defended more than once. At such times, you have to count the attacking and the defending pieces!

In the diagram below, the white e5-knight is attacked by the queen and e8-rook but defended by the e1-rook and d4-pawn. To be able to win a piece, a player usually needs to have more attacking pieces than there are defenders.

If Black plays 1...Bd6, he has an extra attacker and is threatening: 2...Bxe5 3 dxe5 (or 3 Rxe5 Rxe5 4 dxe5 Qxe5, winning a pawn) 3...Rxe5, winning a pawn. White must move the knight or protect it once more. The retreat 2 Nf3 is possible or the defences 2 f4 (the simplest and maybe the best), 2 Qe2, 2 Qe3, 2 Qf4 (all three put the queen in a dangerous position) or 2 Qg5.

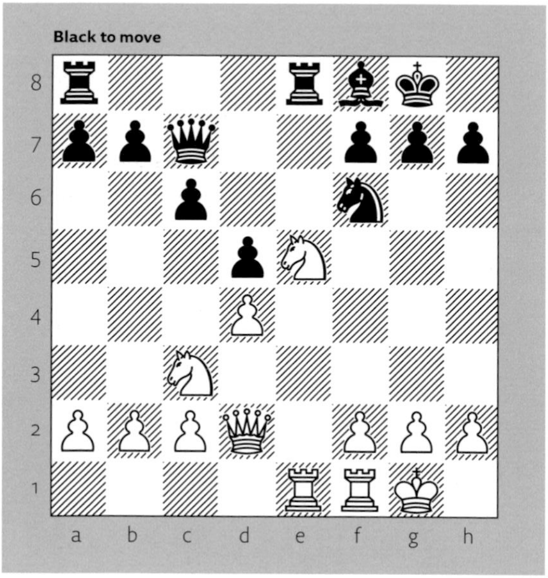

Black to move

The e5-knight is very well placed and so, naturally, Black wants to remove it. Black could also try 1...Nd7 with similar ideas to those above but also threatening 2...f6, forcing the knight to move.

Calculating exchanges

Sometimes it isn't enough just to have more attacking pieces than your opponent, as we can see in these examples.

In both of the positions shown, White has two pieces attacking the knight to Black's single defender and yet, taking the knight will lose material. In the left-hand position, after 1 Rxb6? axb6 2 Rxb6, White has lost a rook for a knight and a pawn. In the right-hand position, 1 Qxg5?? Bxg5 2 Rxg5 and White has lost his queen for knight and bishop.

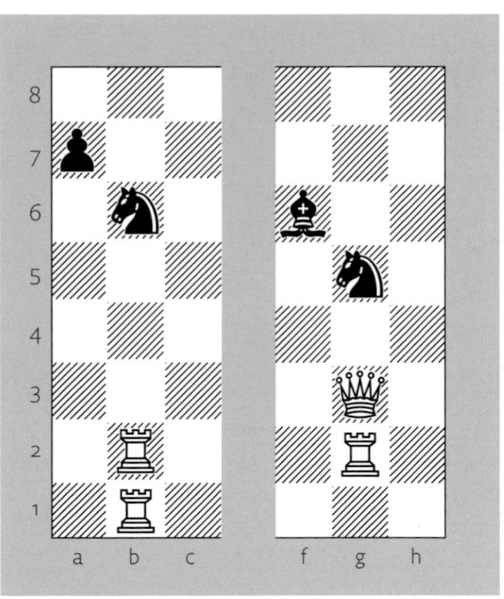

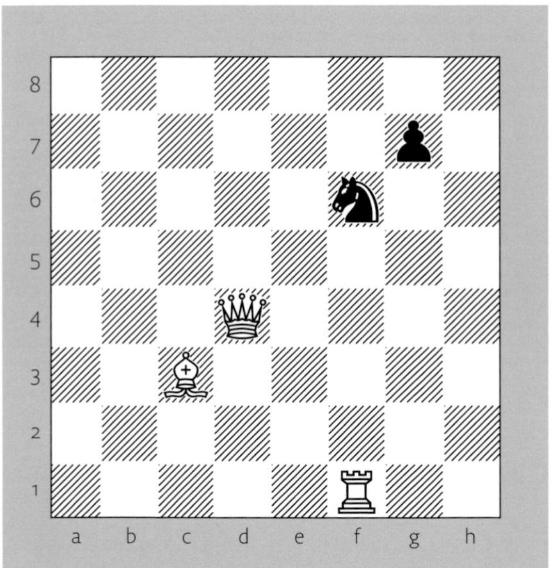

Here White has three pieces attacking the knight to Black's one defender, but both 1 Rxf6? and 1 Qxf6?? are bad moves, losing material.

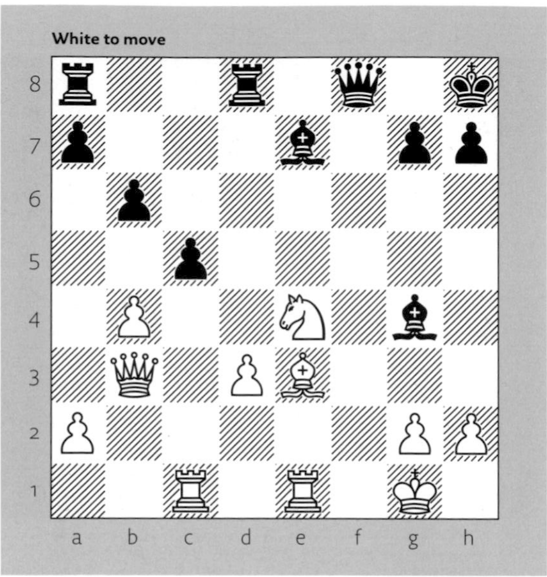

Another two examples to show that counting pieces alone is not enough.

This time White can win a pawn because he has four attackers aimed at c5 and Black has only three defenders (don't forget the black queen). 1 bxc5 bxc5 2 Nxc5 (or 2 Bxc5) and even if Black takes again, White will still have a defended piece on c5, so the black queen must not capture. White has won a pawn.

This position is similar but different in important ways. White still has four attackers aimed at c5 and Black has only three defenders. 1 bxc5 bxc5 2 Nxc5? Bxc5+?? 3 Qxc5 and White has won a pawn, but after 2...Rac8! the knight is pinned, and lost.

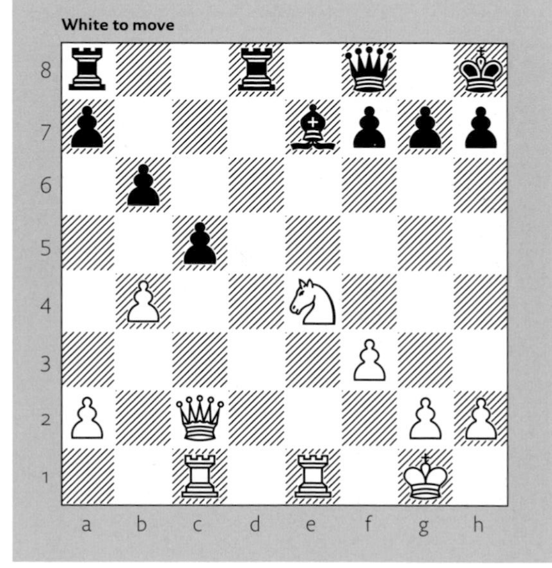

Threats of checkmate

A threat of checkmate is nearly as strong as a check – it's something that can rarely be ignored. It's another thing you have to keep in mind when making your calculations.

The knight is attacked twice and defended only once but White cannot win a pawn by 1 Bxd4 cxd4 2 Rxd4?? because of 2...Re1 mate! The position of the white king in the corner is a strong clue to the risk of mate.

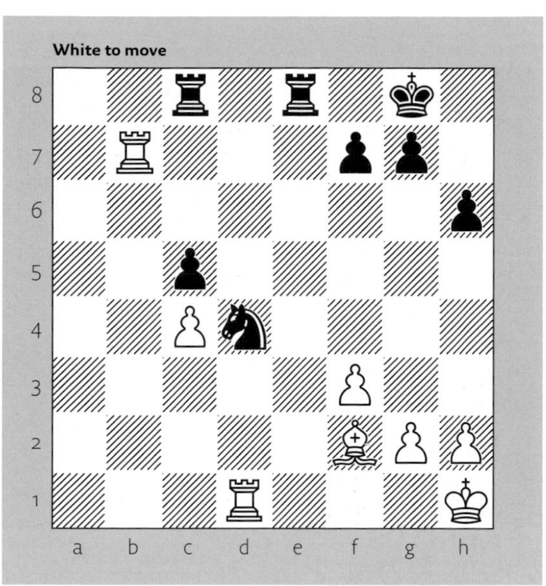

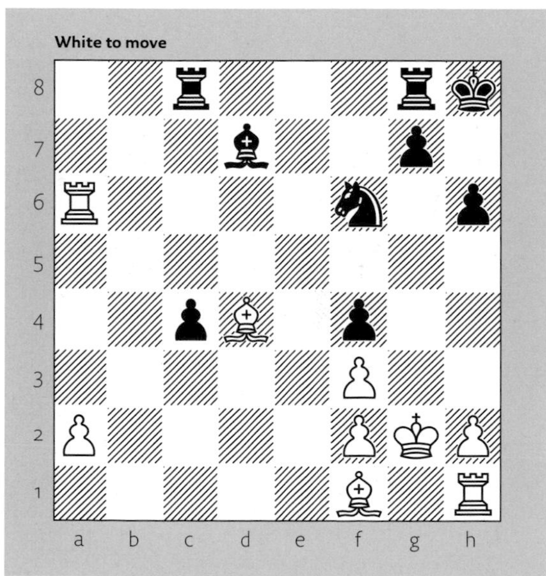

Once again, a black knight is attacked twice and only defended once, but any attempt to win a pawn by capturing twice on f6 meets with a nasty surprise – 1 Bxf6?? gxf6 mate!

3 Winning pieces

To win a game you will almost certainly have to win some of your opponent's pieces. Beginners often give their pieces away, but later when they become more used to how everything moves, this is less common. At this point you will have to employ some of the many devices for winning pieces by force. It's fun, as you will see from the explanations and examples given in this chapter.

Forks

The idea of a fork is simple, you attack two or more pieces at once. Your opponent can save one of them, then you take the other. Here are examples of forks for each of the pieces.

A pawn fork

White plays his pawn to attack both rook and knight. Black can choose which one to move to safety (probably the rook because it is more valuable) and White takes the other.

The moves are: 1 b4 Rb5 2 bxc5 Rxc5. White has won a knight for a pawn.

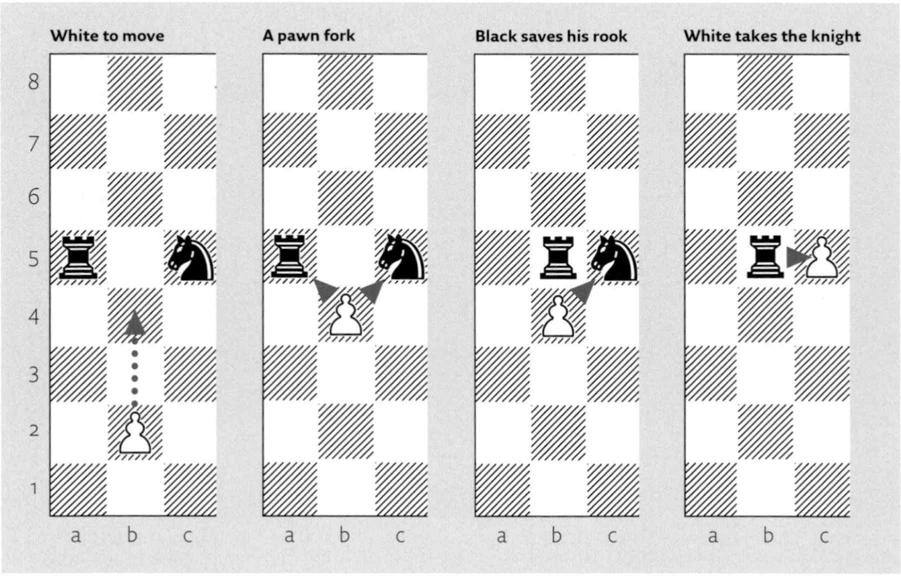

A bishop fork

When two enemy pieces are on the same diagonal, a bishop fork is possible.

If the white bishop moves to b5 it can attack both black pieces. Black's queen cannot sensibly take the bishop or the pawn because they protect one another. Black will save the queen but cannot move it to protect the knight which White will take next move. So Black moves the queen to a square from which it will be able to take the white pawn (a2, b3, b4 or c2).

The moves, as shown below, are: 1 Bb5 Qb4 2 Bxc6 Qxc4. White must now save his bishop and he will then have won a knight for a pawn.

did you know?

Family forks
Knights and queens (and very occasionally rooks and bishops can attack more than two enemy pieces at the same time. These are called 'family forks'.

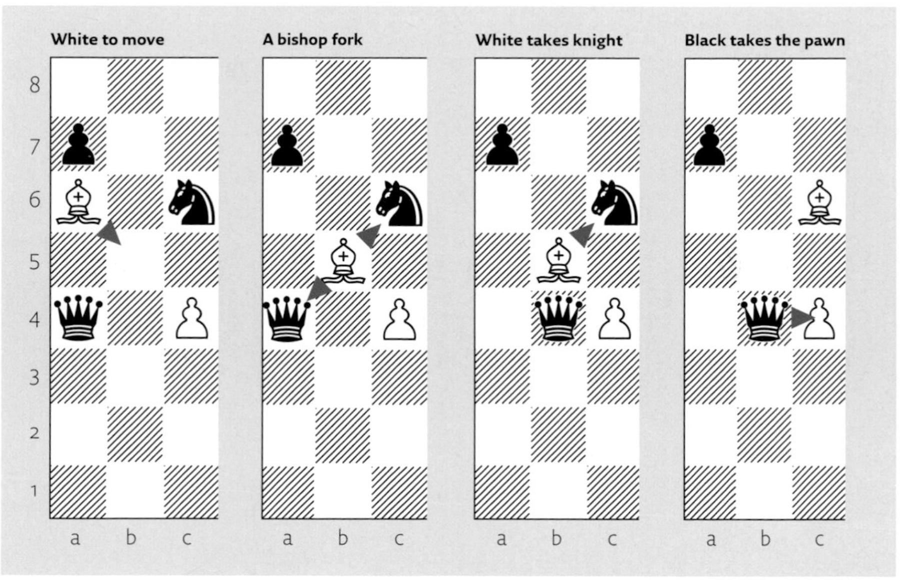

A rook fork

Two unprotected enemy pieces on the same rank or file must beware of a rook fork. You can foresee such possibilities by being aware of undefended pieces.

The rook moves to b5, attacking both white pieces. White chooses to save the bishop by moving it to c2 and Black then takes the knight.

The moves are: 1...Rb5 2 Bc2 Rxb8 and Black has won a knight.

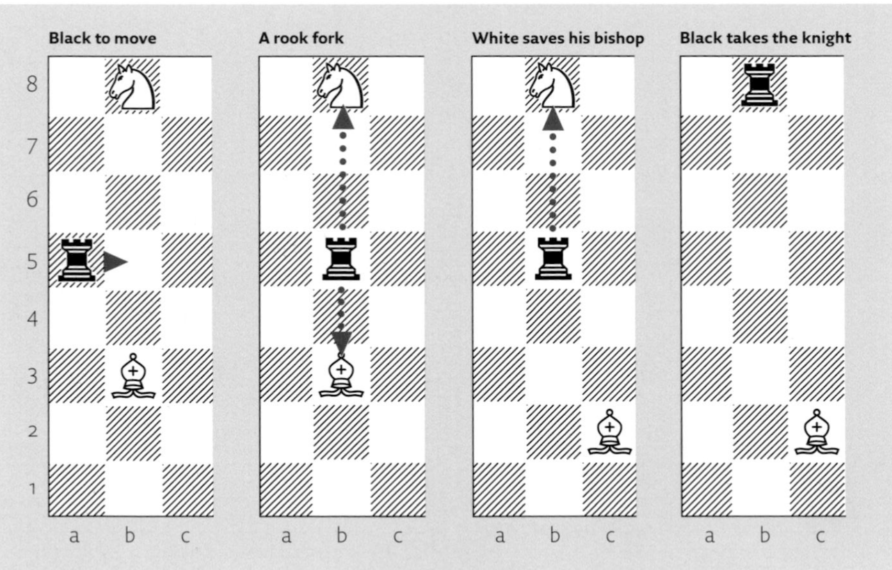

good to know

Alternative moves

In chess you often have a choice of more than one move. In the above example, White could choose to save the knight instead of the bishop. The moves might be: 1...Rb5 2 Nc6 Rxb3.

A queen fork

Queens are always on the lookout for undefended pieces. Because of their great attacking powers, they have frequent chances to win stray pieces.

Black's queen moves to b2, attacking the rook and the knight. White moves the rook away and the queen takes the knight.

The moves are: 1...Qb2 2 Ra4 Qxb6. Black has won a knight.

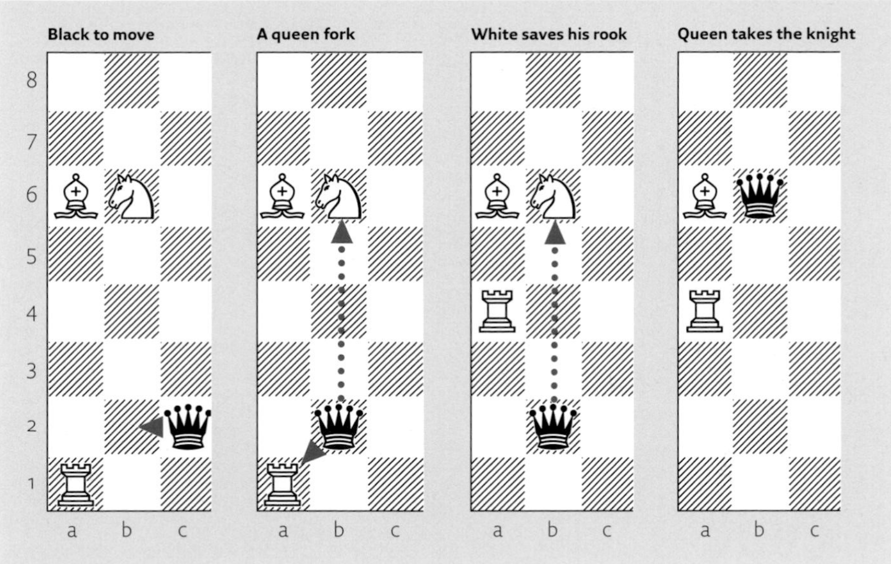

did you know?

Queen power

A queen in the centre of the board can attack up to 27 squares – nearly half the board! This means that very few undefended pieces are safe from the queen, even if it stands in the far corner of the board.

good to know

Those strange knights

The unusual move of the knights takes time to get used to. One tip to help you spot knight forks is that a knight can only fork pieces that stand on the same colour square. A knight always moves from a square of one colour to a square of the other colour. So a knight on a white square can only attack pieces on black squares and vice versa.

A knight fork

The knight is a close rival to the queen for the title of champion when it comes to playing forks. The knight's unusual move seems especially designed for this manoeuvre.

The white knight is attacked by the queen but after it moves to c4 it forks both black pieces. Black saves his queen by moving it to a square where it defends the rook. The knight takes the rook and the queen will then take the knight.

The moves are: 1 Nc4 Qa6 (1...Qa7, 1...Qb4, 1...Qb3 and 1...Qc5 also work, but not 1...Qa5 or 1...Qb2 because those squares are also attacked by the knight) 2 Nxa3 Qxa3. White has won a rook for a knight (this is called 'the exchange', see page 75).

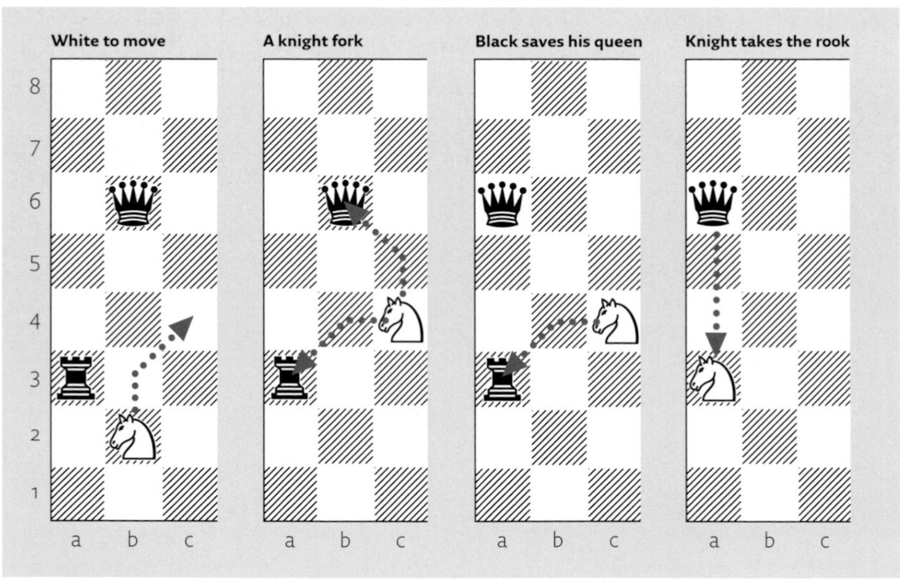

A king fork

Forks by the king are unusual but they occasionally happen, especially if the king is used aggressively when there are few pieces left.

The king moves to b2, attacking both rook and pawn. White moves the rook away and the king takes the pawn.

The moves are: 1...Kb2 2 Rd1 Kxa2. Black has won a pawn.

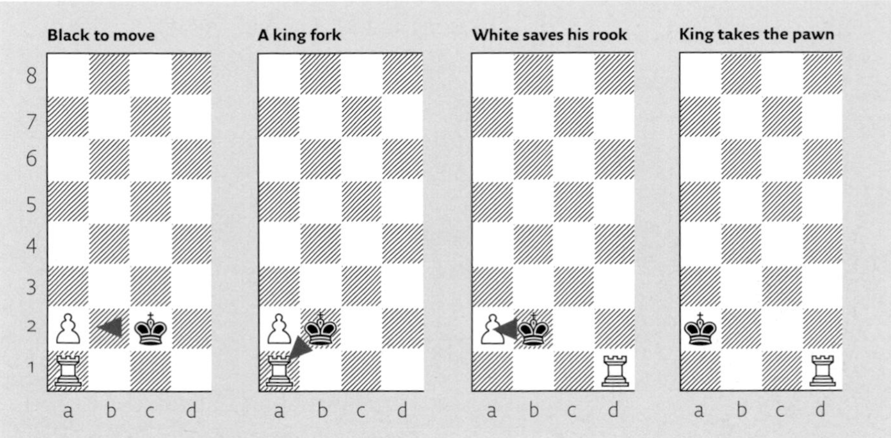

did you know?

The attacking king

Remember, late in the game, when it is safe for him to emerge, the king is an important attacking piece.

Skewers

A skewer is a different way of attacking two opposing pieces at once. The skewer is a long range threat along a rank, file or diagonal, so it is not available to pawns, knights or kings.

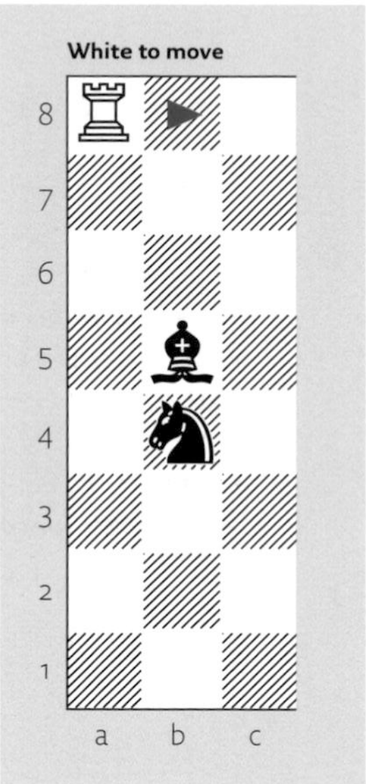

Attacking with skewers

The rook moves to b8 (left), placing the bishop under attack, but if the bishop moves, then the knight is lost. White wins a piece.

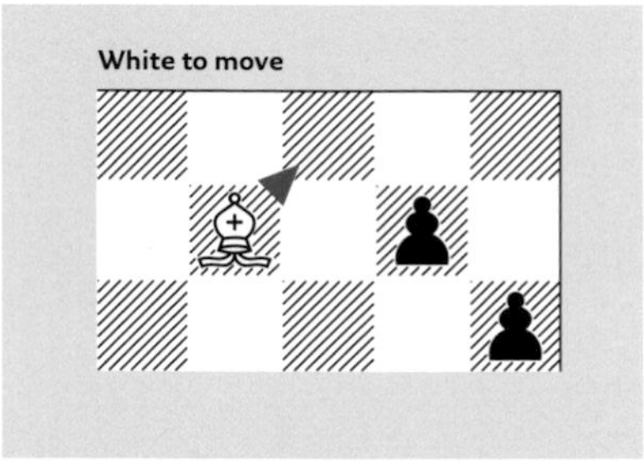

The bishop moves to f8 (above), placing the g7-pawn under attack. If that pawn moves, then the h6 pawn is lost. White wins a pawn.

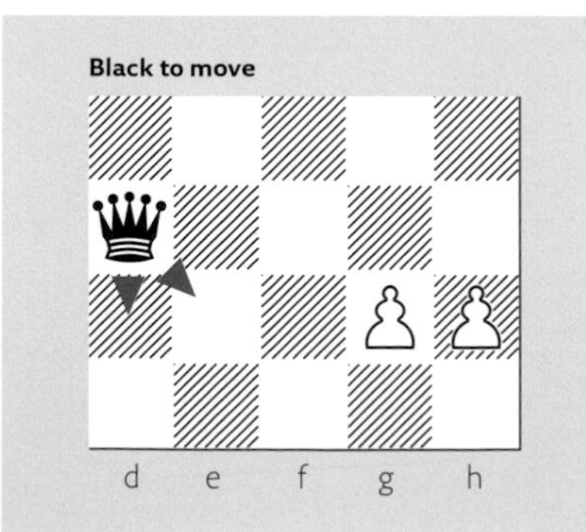

If the queen moves to d2, or e2 (left), then the pawns are skewered. If White moves the g-pawn, the h-pawn is lost. Black wins a pawn.

Double attacks

Another way of threatening two enemy pieces at once, using two of your pieces, is a double attack. One piece moves with a direct attack and, at the same time, reveals an attack by another piece.

Double attacks in action

The white rook, white bishop and black knight are all in line. If the bishop moves, then the rook will be attacking the knight. So, the idea is to find a bishop move that will attack a second enemy piece, as there will then be two black pieces under attack – a 'double attack'.

If White plays 1 Bg8 or 1 Bd3 then Black will move the attacked knight and the bishop will take the h7-pawn.

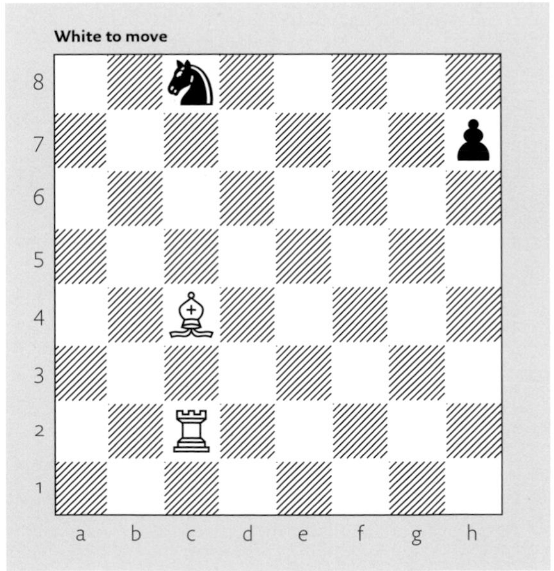

good to know

The latent threat

Double attacks are powerful and often win pieces. The best way to see them in advance is to be aware of latent threats – dangerous alignments of pieces, for example, the rook and the knight in the diagram on this page. Of course, if the knight was protected, the double attack wouldn't work.

must know

Seeing the danger
An experienced player would avoid having his queen on the same diagonal as the enemy bishop, as in the diagram below. As soon as the position arose, he would assess the danger and make plans to move his queen somewhere safer.

Another double attack

Look for a white piece that is lined up against a black piece.

The white bishop is on the same diagonal as the black queen. Any move by the white rook will leave the black queen under attack. Notice that the white knight protects the white bishop. Which is the best square for the white rook?

If White plays 1 Rc7 then, after the black queen moves to safety, White can take the b7-pawn. The moves are: 1 Rc7 Q moves 2 Rxb7, winning a pawn.

However, White has a much better move: 1 Rc8! Black could take this rook in three different ways, but in doing so Black would lose the queen. If Black moves the queen, then White plays 2 Rxa8 and wins a rook. Black could play 1...Rxc8 2 Bxf6 gxf6 or 1...Qxb2 2 Nxb2 Rxc8 when White has won a queen for a rook and a bishop.

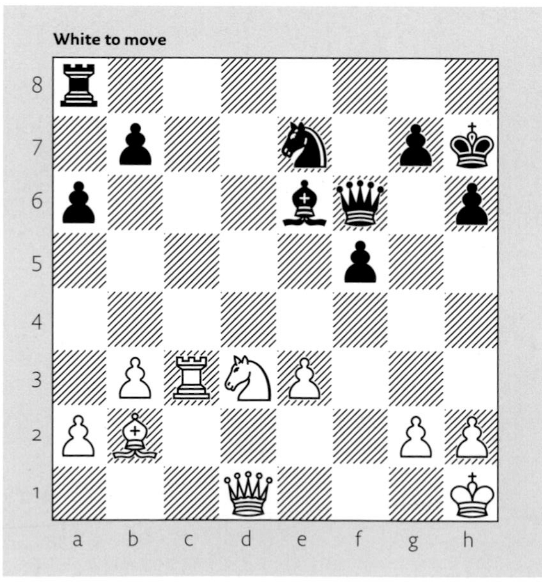

Winning ways with check

All of the methods (forks, skewers and double attacks) of threatening and winning enemy pieces can also be played with an attack on the enemy king – a check.

More powerful

Checks are an even more powerful way of using these tactical ideas because your opponent must get out of check and this means less choice of moves.

White plays 1 Rb1+ (skewer) and will win the black pawn on b7 after the king moves out of check.

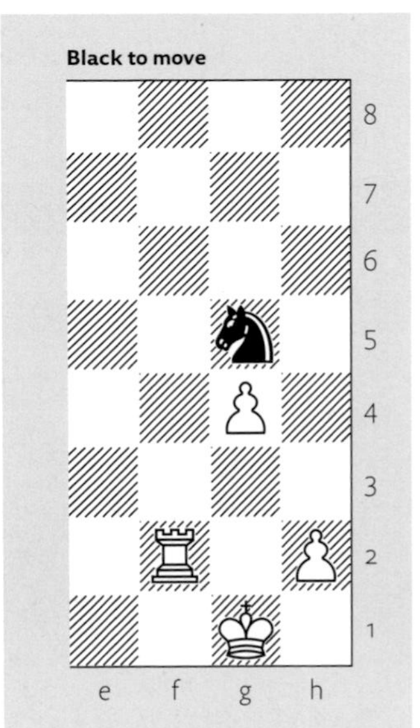

Black plays 1...Nh3+ (fork) and will take the rook next move after the king moves out of check to f1 or g2 (from where it still defends its rook). 2...Nxf2 3 Kxf2 and Black has won the exchange (a rook for a knight).

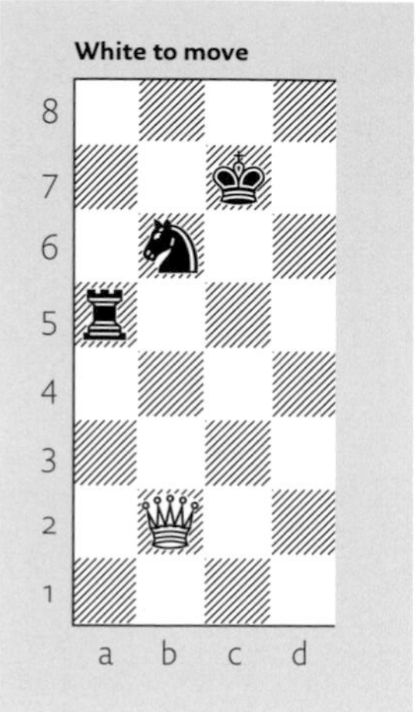

Above: 1 Qc1+ and 1 Qc2+ are just checks, but 1 Qc3+ (fork) also attacks the rook and wins it. The moves are: 1 Qc3+ Kb7 2 Qxa5.

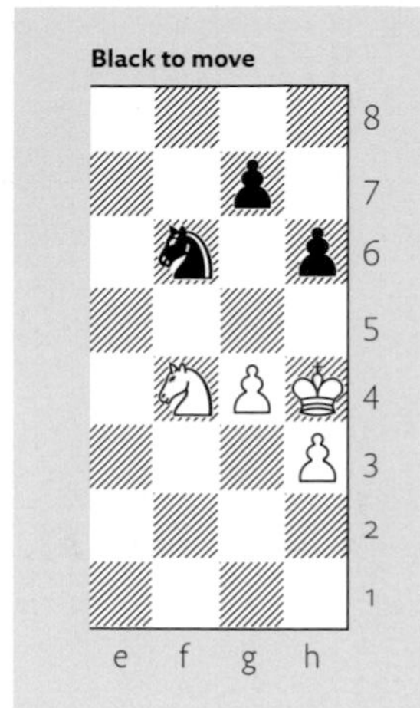

Above: 1...g5+ (fork) attacks both king and knight. The pawn is protected by the h6-pawn. White must reply 2 Kg3 and play continues, 2...gxf4+ 3Kxf4, but Black has won a knight for a pawn.

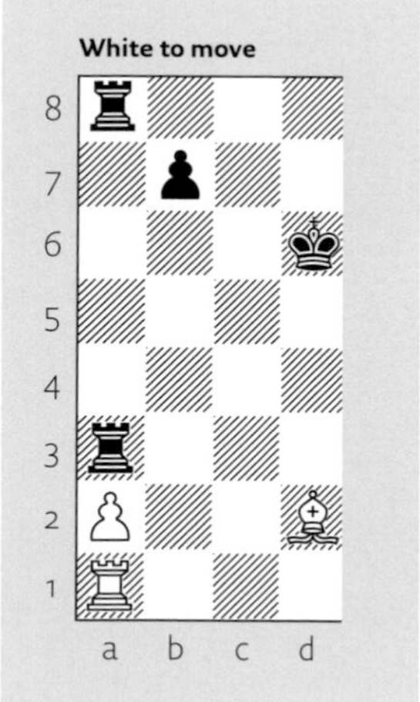

Above: White plays the bishop fork 1 Bb4+ and after the black king moves out of check, 2 Bxa3. After 2...Rxa3, White has won a rook for a bishop (called 'the exchange').

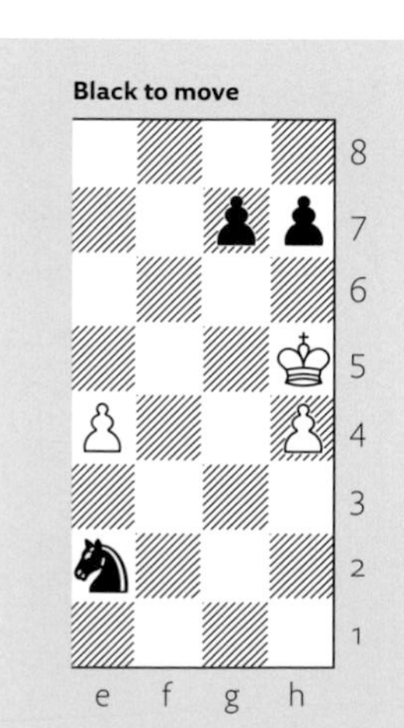

Left: Black wins a pawn by playing 1...Ng3+ (fork) and after the king moves out of check, then 2...Nxe4.

More about double checks

The only way out of a double check is a king move because you cannot take two checking pieces at once, nor block two checks at once. That's why a double check is so powerful. It is a special form of the double attack.

watch out!

Take care
All checks can be dangerous, so be especially careful whenever an enemy piece is lined up on your king, even when there are other pieces in between.

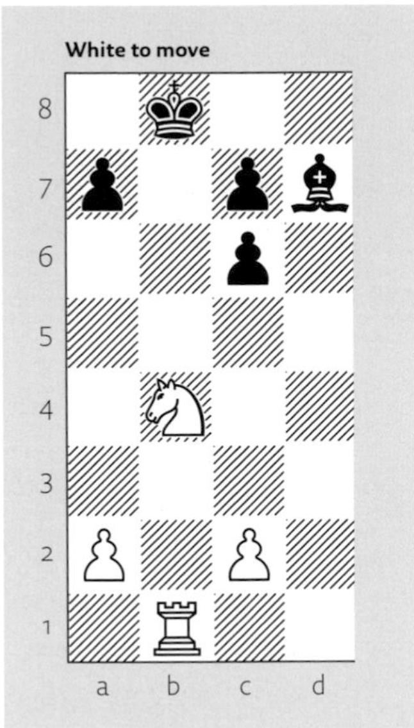

White plays 1 Nxc6+, a double check from rook and knight. Black can only play 1...Ka8 or 1...Kc8 and in both cases White replies 2 Rb8 mate! 1 Na6+ gives exactly the same result.

Black plays 1...Nxf3+, again a double check, this time from knight and bishop, forcing the white king to move. Black can then continue with 2...Nxg1. This shows just how powerful the double check is.

Pins

As the name suggests a pin is a tactic that 'pins down' one piece to another. If a piece is pinned to the king, you are not allowed to move it because any move would place the king in check.

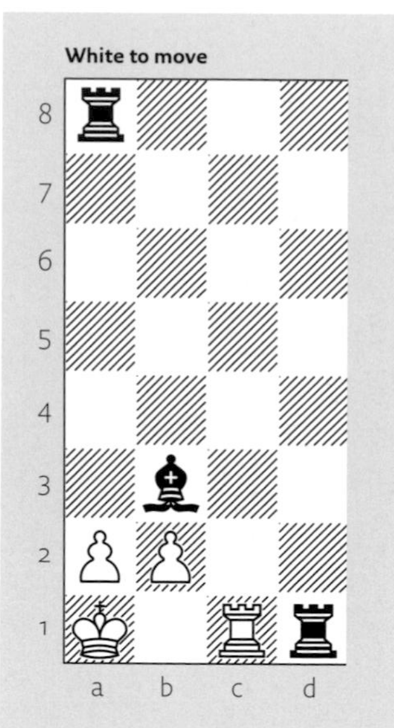

A pinned pawn

The a2-pawn cannot take the bishop (1 axb3) because that would leave the white king in check from the black rook. The pawn can move to a3 (or a4, but then it would just be taken). In this situation the a2-pawn is said to be 'pinned'. The white rook on c1 is also pinned by the black rook on d1. The white rook can take the black rook or move to b1 but it cannot move along the c-file as that would put the white king in check.

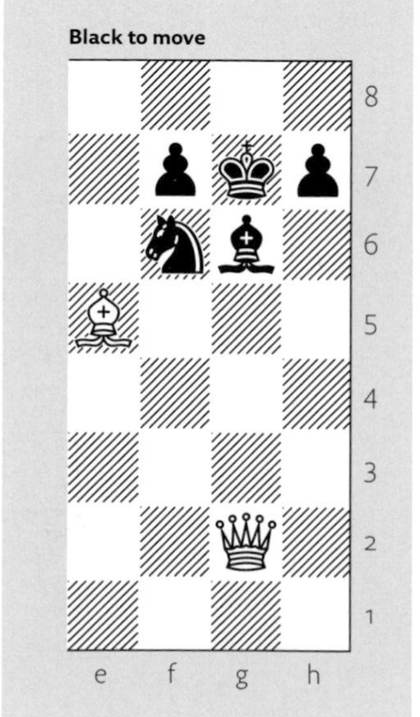

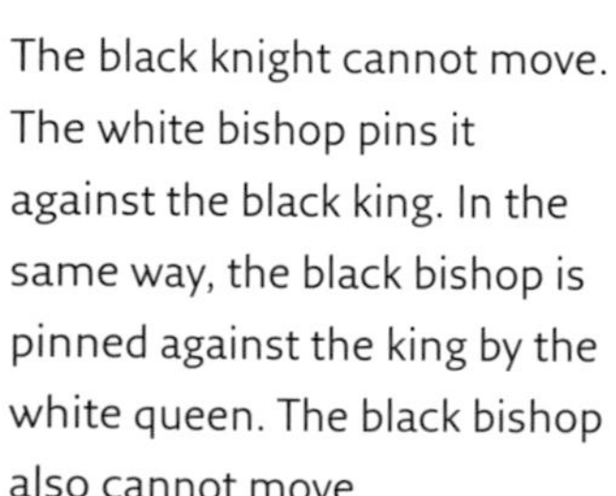
The black knight cannot move. The white bishop pins it against the black king. In the same way, the black bishop is pinned against the king by the white queen. The black bishop also cannot move.

Another kind of pin

In these cases, it is legal to move the pinned piece because the pin is against an ordinary piece not the king. However, ignoring the pin is not a good idea as you will see.

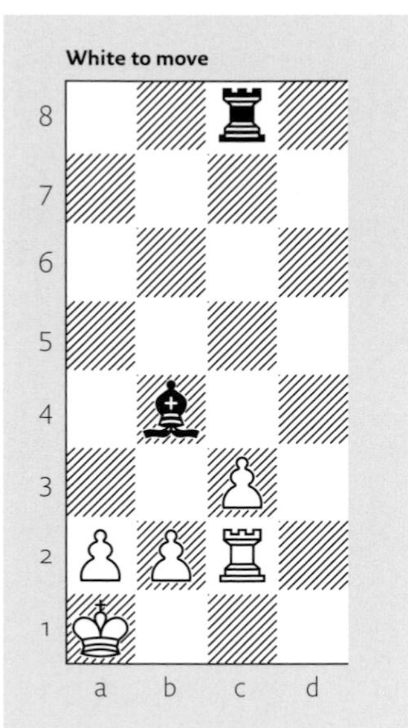

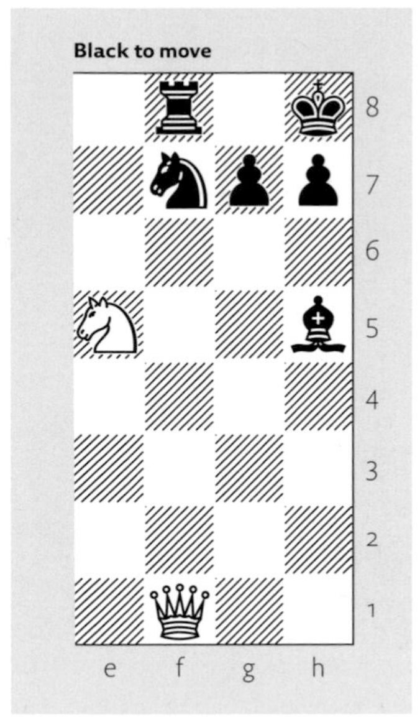

The black rook on c8 pins the white c3-pawn because of the unprotected rook on c2. If White played 1 cxb4 then Black would reply 1...Rxc2 and win the exchange. The pawn capture is possible (legal), but it is a bad move because it loses the rook for the bishop.

The white queen pins the knight on f7 because of the unprotected rook on f8. If Black plays 1...Nxe5, for example, then 2 Qxf8 is mate! The knight move is legal, but is not advisable.

Why pins are important

Anything which restricts your choice of moves is bad. It makes things harder for you and easier for your opponent. Let's see what can happen to a pinned (restricted) piece.

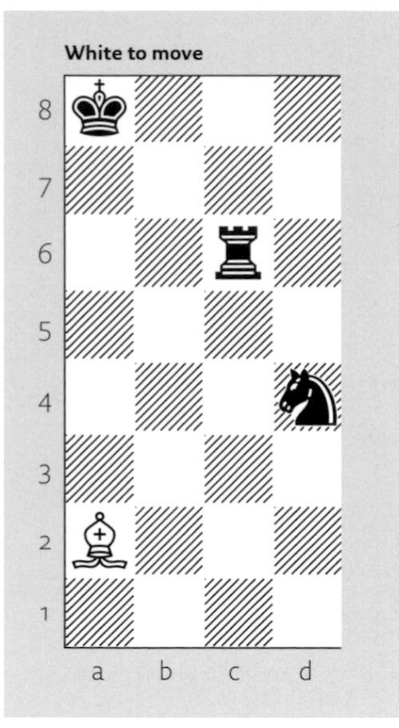

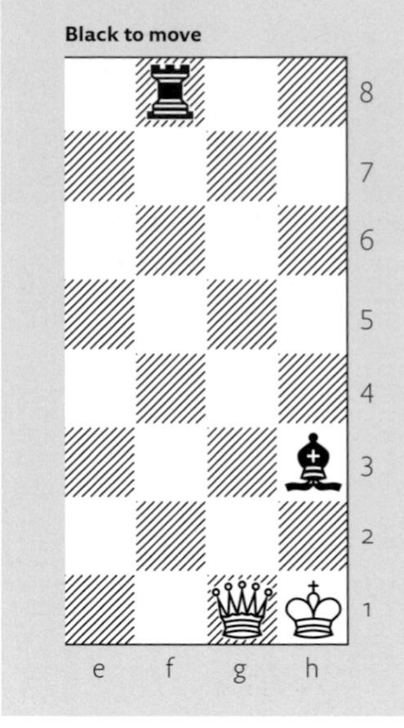

The black rook and king are on the same diagonal. After White plays 1 Bd5, the black rook cannot move because it is pinned to the king. The fact that the rook is protected by the knight does not help. White will take the rook next move and will have won the exchange (a rook for a bishop), if the bishop is then taken by the black knight.

The white queen and king are in line. After Black plays 1...Rf1 the white queen cannot move because it is pinned to the king. This enables the black rook to capture it next move. Even though the white king can then take the rook, Black will have won a queen for a rook.

Attacking pinned pieces

The white bishop is pinned by the black rook, but the bishop is protected twice by the f3-pawn and the king. However, the protectors cannot help the bishop after 1...f5. Because it cannot move, it will be lost, for example: 2 Kxg6 fxg4 and Black has won a bishop for a pawn.

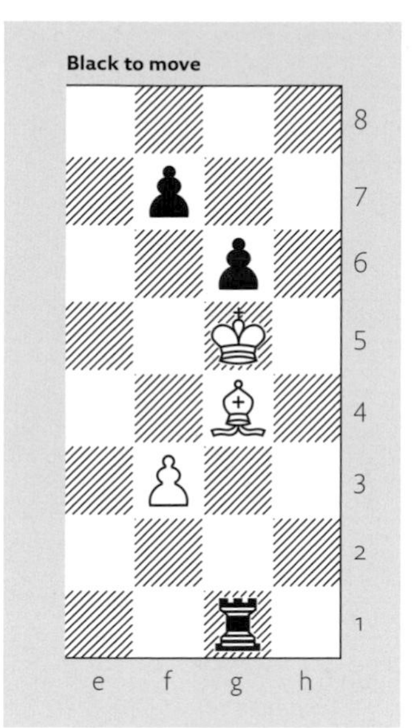

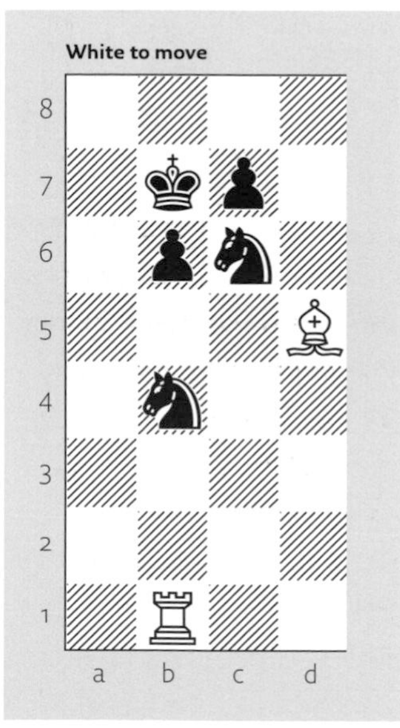

Pinned pieces cannot defend

White can play 1 Rxb4 and Black cannot recapture because the c6-knight is pinned by the d5-bishop.

did you know?

Pin priorities

- One of the unofficial 'rules' of chess is always attack a pinned piece.
- If one of your pieces is pinned then getting out of the pin is usually a high priority. It is even better to avoid the pin in the first place.

Winning in the middlegame

In this book you will find plenty of examples of how to go about winning your opponent's pieces. These examples form a vital part of the game. They are also one of the most enjoyable and understandable parts of chess.

Attacking and exchanging

If you are under attack, try to exchange pieces. If you are attacking, avoid exchanging pieces if you can.

If there is no attack, then exchange if you have more pieces. It is generally better to have two pieces against one rather than five against four.

Bring all of your pieces into play. Move them towards the centre of the board where they are more powerful. Always be on the look-out for better squares for your pieces.

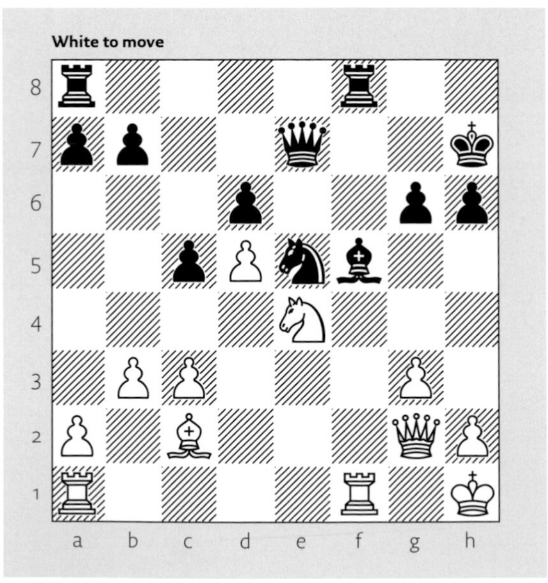

The a1-rook is still not part of the game in the diagram on the left, so if you have nothing else definite, play 1 Rae1 which brings the rook into the game, defends the knight again and puts the rook opposite the enemy queen – a possible pin on the black knight.

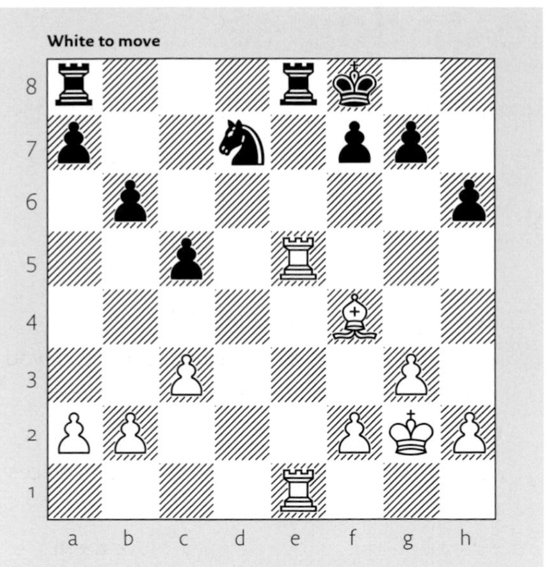

In the above diagram White's rooks are definitely in the game. They illustrate the power of doubled rooks. White can continue 1 Rxe8+ Rxe8 2 Bd6+ (forcing away the king) 2...Kg8 3 Rxe8+. White has won a rook.

watch out!

Improving your rooks

Watch out for 'the lazy queen's rook'. It isn't really the queen's rook that's lazy, it's you who forgets to bring it into the game. Rooks love open files (files without pawns) and they work together very well (two rooks on one file are called 'doubled rooks').

Winning in the endgame

Every beginner needs to learn how to checkmate the enemy king with just his king and one major piece. The big danger is giving stalemate instead of checkmate!

watch out!

There are dangers
When checkmating with king and rook, keep your rook protected. Always watch out for stalemates (see page 63).

Forcing checkmate

How can you force checkmate with king and queen against king? You need to:

a) use your queen to force the enemy king to the side of the board;

b) bring up your king to help force checkmate;

c) beware of stalemates!

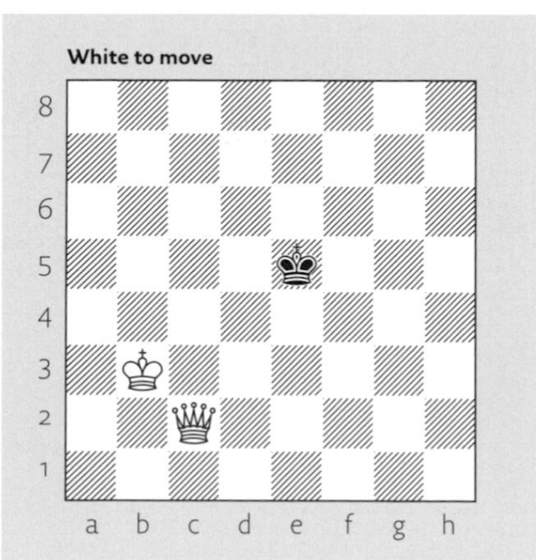

In this situation White could play: 1 Qc4 Kd6 2 Qb5 Ke6 3 Qc5 Kf6 4 Qd5 Ke7 5 Qc6 Kf7 6 Qd6 Kg7 7 Qe6 Kh7 8 Qf6 Kg8 9 Qe7. White has now achieved stage 'a', above. The black king can only move between g8 and h8. Stage 'b' is for White to march his king to f6 and then play Qg7 mate.

Note that the white queen did not give check in achieving stage 'a'. On every move the black king gave way and the queen moved to create a smaller space for the king.

Now put a white rook on c2 instead of the queen. The big difference is that the white king must stay with the rook in order to protect it.
1 Rc4 Kd5 2 Kc3 Ke5 3 Rd4 Kf5 4 Kd3 Ke5 5 Ke3 Ke6 6 Ke4 Kf6 7 Rd5 Ke6 8 Kd4 Ke7 9 Ke5 Kf7 10 Rd6 Ke7 11 Kd5 Kf7 12 Re6 Kg7 13 Ke5 Kf7 14 Kf5 Kf8 15 Kg6 Kg8 16 Re8 mate.

Winning with bishops

Checkmating with two bishops is more difficult and needs practice. The steps are:

a) keep your bishops together and close to the centre of the board;

b) force the enemy king into a corner of the board using your king;

c) beware of stalemates!

1 Bb4+ Kf1 2 Bc4+ Kg1 3 Kg3 Kh1 4 Bb5 (This is just to waste a move. You want a position in which the white king isn't blocking the key diagonals and you can play a check forcing the black king into the corner, as on move 5.) 4...Kg1 (this is the position you need) 5 Bc5+ Kh1 6 Bc6 mate.

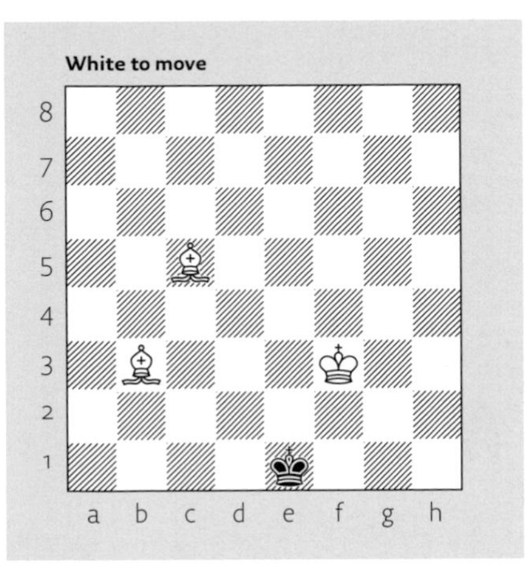

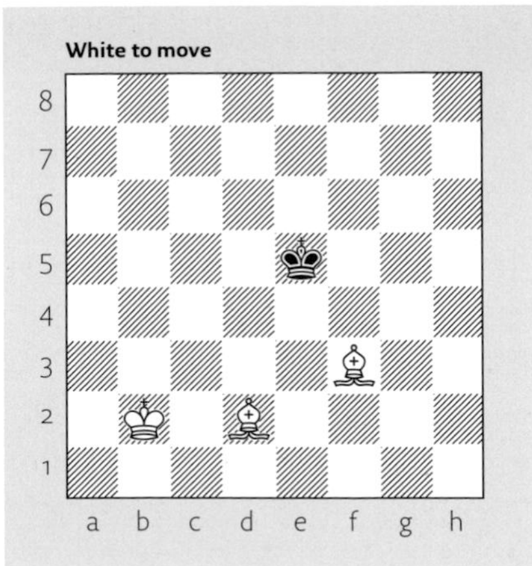

Now try to force mate in the left-hand diagram, following the general principles set out above. It isn't easy!

It is possible to checkmate with king, bishop and knight against a lone king, but it hardly ever crops up, is extremely difficult and very few players know how to do it. Some things we can leave alone.

good to know

Kings and pawns only
Endings with only kings and pawns are quite rare. If the enemy king is close enough to your advanced pawn to stop it promoting, then you will need to advance your own king to keep your pawn protected.

Winning by promoting pawns

Neither side has the pieces to checkmate so both players must play to promote a pawn.

Look for a part of the board where you have more pawns and try to advance a pawn that does not have an enemy pawn in front of it.

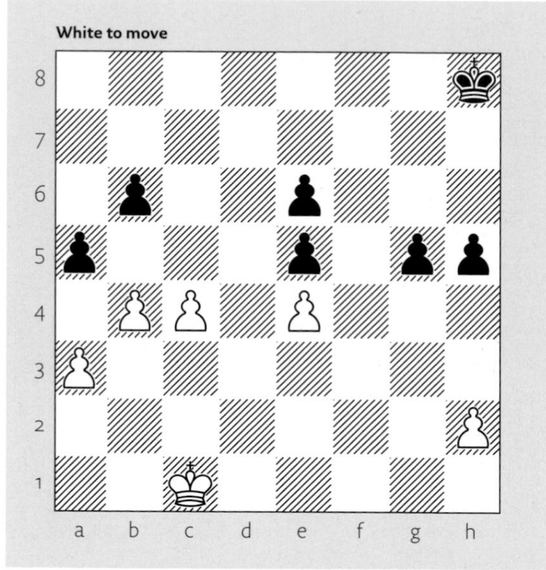

1 c5! bxc5 2 bxc5 (White now has a 'passed pawn', that is, a pawn that doesn't have to get past another pawn in order to queen, see page 148) 2...g4 (the black king cannot get to the c-pawn before it queens, so Black tries to make a queen of his own) 3 c6 h4 4 c7 g3 5 c8Q+ and White will win easily by stopping the black king's side pawns (for example, 5...Kg7 6 hxg3 hxg3 7 Qxe6 g2 8 Qg4+ wins the g-pawn).

More winning ways

This example shows the difference between the powers of a knight and a bishop. The knight is a short distance piece but it can attack all squares, whereas the bishop is a long distance piece that can attack squares of only one colour. Black's bishop cannot defend its pawns on the queen's side and the king is too far away to do the job. The bishop must attack the white queen's side pawns instead.

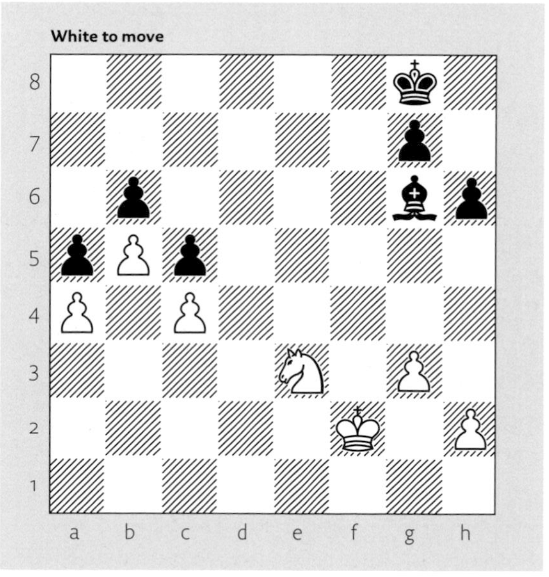

1 Nd5 (a good central square for the knight which maximizes its strength; Black cannot defend the pawn on b6) 1...Bc2 (if Black attacks the c4-pawn by 1...Bd3 or 1...Bf7, the result is similar) 2 Nxb6 (and the knight defends both the a4- and c4-pawns) 2...Kf7 3 Nd7 Bxa4 4 Nxc5 Bc2 5 b6 and there is no way for Black to stop the advance of the b-pawn.

Forcing mate

'Never miss a check, it might be mate!' is a famous chess maxim. It does not mean that you should play every check that arises, but consider every one in case it leads to something even better.

good to know

Chess talk

The world of chess has a language of its own. One of its peculiarities is that no-one uses the word 'checkmate'. It is usually abbreviated to 'mate'.

Examples

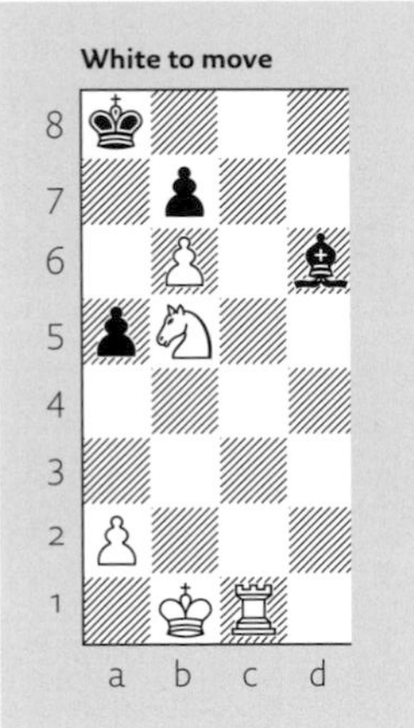

The king is trapped on the back rank. 1 Rc8+ forces 1...Bb8 and then 2 Nc7 is mate (the bishop is pinned).

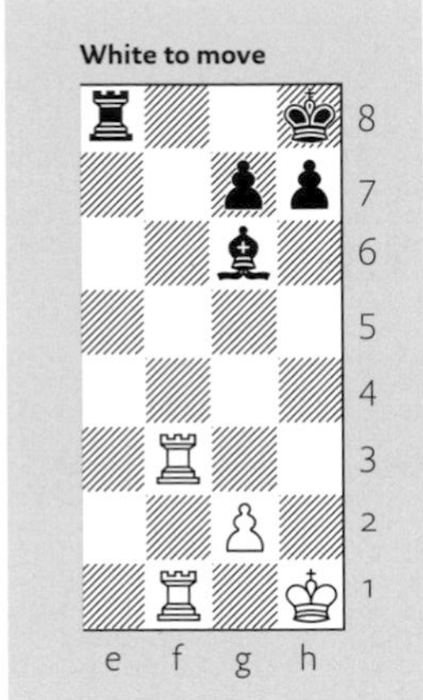

Another trapped king on the back rank. 1 Rf8+ gives Black no choice – 1...Rxf8 and then 2 Rxf8 is mate.

The black king cannot move. 1 Rxe5+ would allow the king to escape, but 1 Bb5+ Nc6 2 Bxc6 is a forced mate.

Checks that lead to mate

Black has not seen the threat to f7 from the bishop and the queen. 1 Qxf7+ Kd7 (forced) 2 Be6 mate! 1 Bxf7+ (hoping for 1...Kd7? 2 Qf5 mate) is not as good because there is no forced mate after 1...Kf8 2 Bd6+ Nf6.

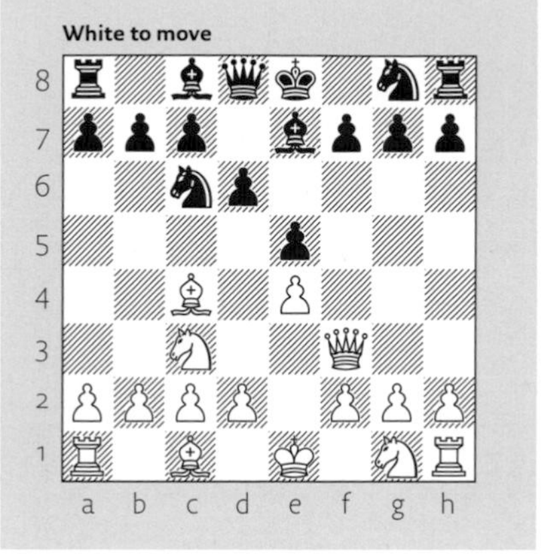

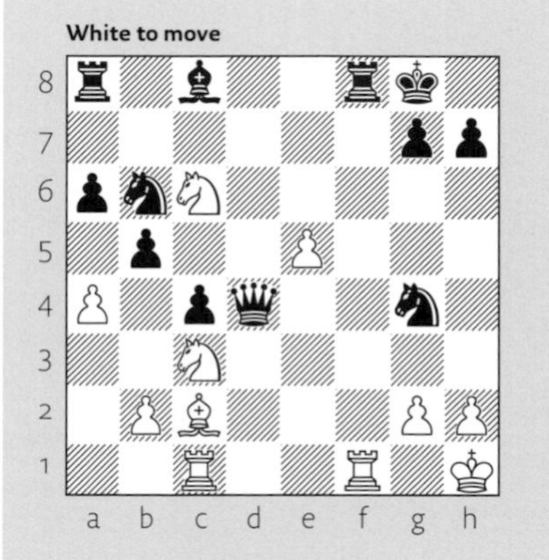

The c6-knight could take the black queen, but 1 Ne7+ Kh8 (forced) 2 Rxf8 mate is better!

1 Nd6+ forces Black to reply 1....Kd8 or 1...Kf8 and then 2 Nxe6 is mate.

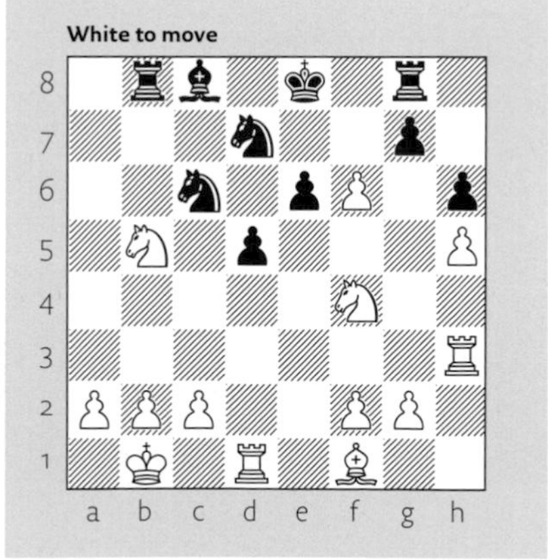

4 Some simple games

Having learned the moves and the basic ideas, it is now time to see some action. In this chapter there is a collection of very short games with elementary mistakes by one side and good play by the other. The mistakes are punished severely and the play is instructive and entertaining. The examples demonstrate many chess tactics and strategies – developing pieces, playing to control the centre and avoiding exposing your king. Enjoy these games and try to avoid the mistakes in your own efforts.

Short and sweet

None of the following games last very long because one player makes an basic error. In the opening the most important thing is to get your pieces into play.

must know

Actual moves

In the games in this section, the moves played are given in bold (heavy) type. Other moves in normal type are alternatives that could, and sometimes should, have been played. Such 'discussions' about the moves help to give the reader a clearer idea of what is happening on the board.

Fool's Mate

This is the shortest possible checkmate:

1 g4 e5 2 f3 Qh4 mate

The diagram shows the final position.

There are three ways to get out of check:

1) take the piece giving check;

2) move the king out of check;

3) block the check by putting a piece between the piece giving check and the king.

Surprisingly, White cannot do any of these, so it is checkmate.

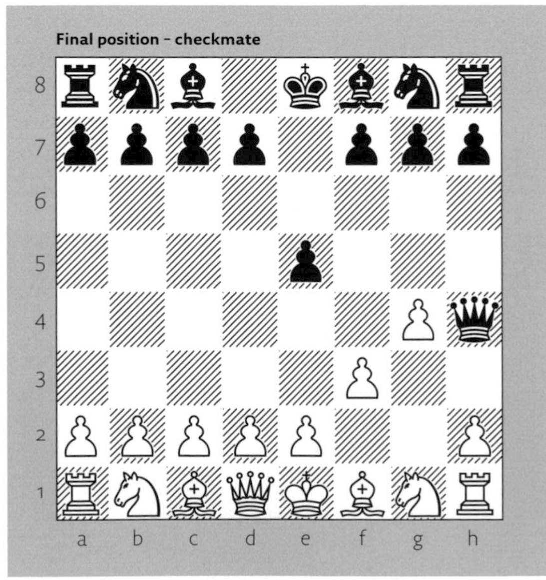

Scholar's Mate

Another quick checkmate, Scholar's Mate, is often seen in school chess – hence its name.

1 e4 e5 2 Bc4 Nc6 3 Qh5 Nf6?? 4 Qxf7 mate

The diagram below illustrates the final position.

Make sure you understand why this position is checkmate. The king cannot take the queen to get out of check because then the c4-bishop would be giving check.

Instead of the blunder on move 3, Black should have played g7-g6 to block the queen's attack on f7, or protected the f7-pawn by Qe7 or Qf6.

Final position – checkmate

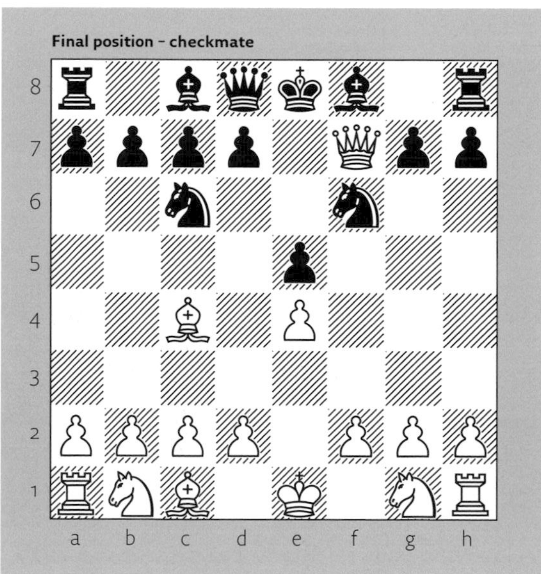

must know

Avoid blunders

The '??' shows that a move is a very serious mistake – known as a 'blunder' (see page 72).

good to know

Playing tips

- Do not expose your king; protect your weak point at f7 or f2 (see below) if it is attacked
- Do not bring your queen out too early
- After you have castled, do not weaken your king's protection.

Weak points

The squares f2 and f7 are the weakest squares on the board at the start of the game. This is because they are only protected by the king. All the other squares in each sides' position are defended by a stronger piece.

good to know

Players
When experienced players get into a very bad position, they sometimes 'resign' the game, because they know their opponent will not make a mistake and fail to win. Your opponents will not be that good and you don't gain experience in that way. Play on until mate!

Setting about winning

In general, there are three ways of achieving checkmate:

1) a direct attack on the enemy king (this may not produce a checkmate but if it enables you to win an enemy piece, then switch to option 2 below);

2) improve the position of your pieces and try to win enemy pieces, so that you have a bigger army, and then attack your opponent's king;

3) if you don't have enough pieces to force a checkmate, try to 'queen' (promote) a pawn and then attack the enemy king.

Let's look at the kinds of mistakes that can happen early.

Your opponent exposes his king

1 d4 f5 2 Bg5 h6?

After this a queen check on h5 will be very dangerous.

3 Bh4 g5??

Black can trap the bishop but doesn't see the danger to his king.

4 Bg3 f4

The bishop is lost. Is the game over? Well, nearly!

5 e3!

Threatening Qh5 mate!

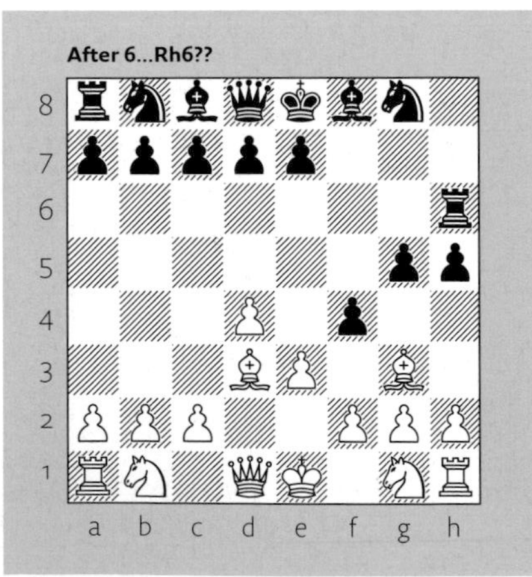

5...h5

5...Nf6, developing a piece, would be a better move. Now White can win a pawn on f4, but even better is:

6 Bd3!

Threatening Bg6 mate! Black must make some space around his king, by Bg7 or e6.

6...Rh6?? (see diagram)

Black has everything defended, but now comes the big surprise.

7 Qxh5+!

What a shock. Black has no choice.

7...Rxh5 8 Bg6 mate!

Endangering the king by exposure

1 e4 e5 2 Nf3 Nf6 3 Nxe5 Nxe4?

(see diagram)

Black should play 3...d6 to drive back the white knight which is in a dangerous attacking position. After 4 Nf3, Black can safely take on e4.

4 Qe2

White immediately attacks the enemy knight and, by occupying the e-file, threatens the black king.

4...Nf6?? (see diagram)

This sets up a discovered check for White. Black needed to play 4...d5 and then, if 5 d3, he could reply 5...Qe7 on a 'you attack my knight and I'll attack yours' basis. It doesn't get him out of trouble because of 6 dxe4 Qxe5 7 exd5 winning a pawn because the black queen is pinned, but it's better than the discovered check!

Now, wherever the knight goes, it will be check. So what do you want to win? 5 Nxf7+? is no good because of 5...Kxf7. 5 Ng6+ wins the rook on h8 but, even better is:

5 Nc6+! (see diagram)

The knight attacks the queen and if 5...Qe7, the knight is still attacking the queen. Opening the e-file has cost Black his queen.

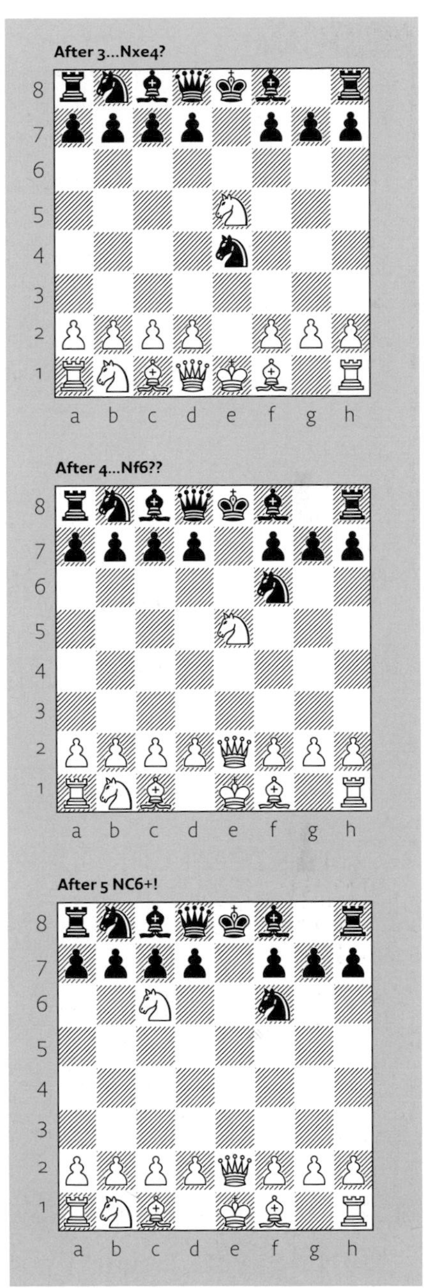

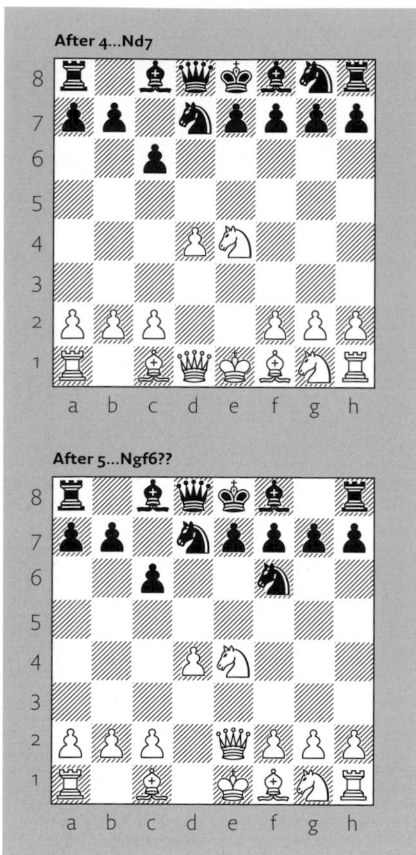

Black surrounds his king

Sometimes the e-file can be fatal even when it still has a pawn on it.

1 e4 c6 2 d4 d5 3 Nc3 dxe4

4 Nxe4 Nd7? (see diagram)

The last move is poor because it leaves the black king surrounded. Black thinks that the king must be safe so early in the game. 4...Nf6 would be a much better move.

5 Qe2

This isn't a good move because the queen blocks the f1-bishop, but it does set a simple trap and Black falls right into it, this time.

5...Ngf6?? (see diagram)

Black doesn't see what's coming.

6 Nd6 mate!

The e-pawn is pinned to the king by the white queen and the black king cannot breathe.

The same idea can come about by 1 e4 e5 2 f4 exf4 3 Nf3 (to stop Qh4+) 3...d5 4 Nc3 dxe4 5 Nxe4 Bg4 6 Qe2 (Black must now play a move that prevents the discovered check, such as 6...Be7, but thinks it's good enough to attack the white queen) 6...Bxf3?? 7 Nf6 mate! It's double check, so the attack on the queen does not matter. Note that 7 Nd6+ isn't good enough because the king can escape to d7.

White surrounds his king

This example of a player surrounding the king is quite bizarre.

1 e4 e6 2 d4 d5 3 Nd2

This seems odd as it blocks the bishop, but White can get away with it. 3 e5, 3 exd5 and 3 Nc3 are all good moves.

3...c5

Because White's last move was rather quiet, Black can afford to attack the centre instead of rushing to get his pieces into play.

4 exd5 exd5 (see diagram)

5 dxc5?

This is poor because it helps Black to develop his bishop to a good square, attacking the weak point f2.

5...Bxc5 6 Ne2?? (see diagram)

Look what he's done to his king (and his bishops)!

6...Qb6! (see diagram)

Black threatens Bxf2 mate and White cannot defend that pawn. White must move a knight to make space for his king. If he moves the d2-knight or tries Nc3, Nf4, Ng3 or Ng1, then 7...Bxf2+ 8 Ke2 Qe3 mate is the answer. White can only play 7 Nd4 Bxd4 8 Qe2+, but has lost a piece in the process.

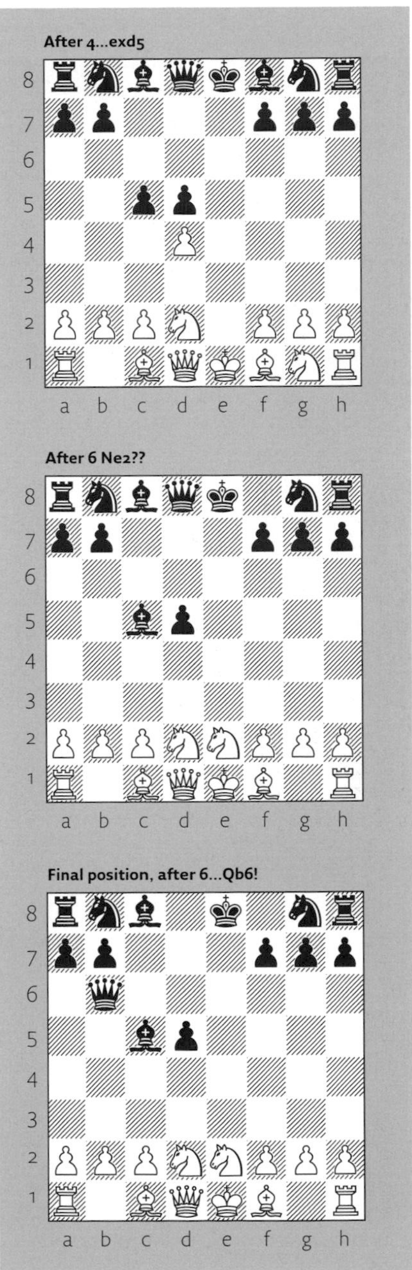

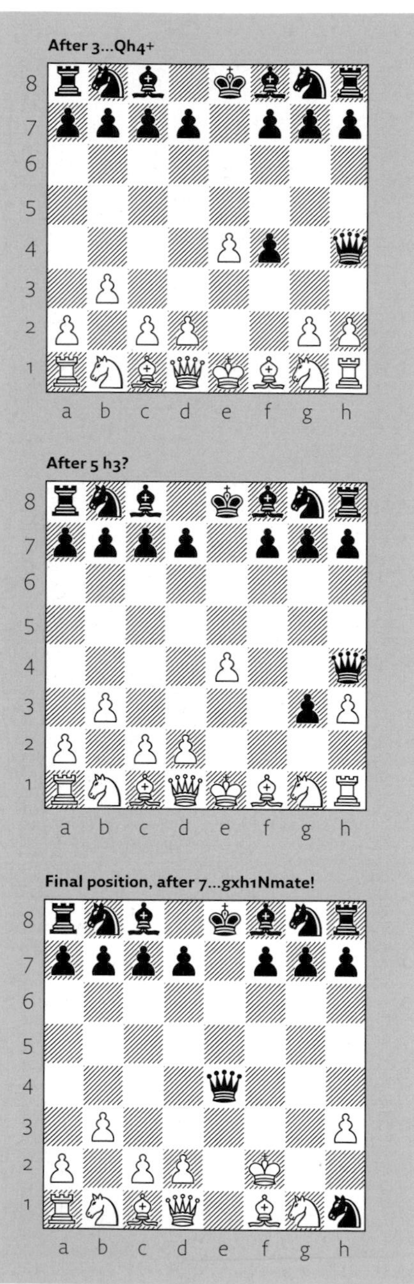

White fails to develop his pieces

This example illustrates a very clever finish by Black, but poor play by White.

1 e4 e5 2 f4 exf4 3 b3?

White needs to develop pieces and to prevent Black's next move. 3 Nf3 would be an advisable move.

3...Qh4+ (see diagram)

White is suddenly in trouble. If the king moves, White will not be able to castle, so...

4 g3 fxg3

Things are getting worse for White. Now the h-pawn is pinned.

5 h3? (see diagram)

This move does prevent 5...gxh2+.

5...g2+!

Black's response is a discovered check from the queen. White's rook is also threatened and he has no choice but to move his king.

6 Ke2

Now Black finds a very neat way to finish.

6....Qxe4+ 7 Kf2 gxh1N mate!

(see diagram)

In this game White has not developed a single piece, unless you count his king.

Black fails to develop his pieces

Here, Black doesn't fail entirely to develop his pieces, but certainly does not put them in useful places.

1 e4 d6 2 Bc4

Threatening the weak f7.

2...Nd7

The knight is not as active here as it would be at c6 and it is blocking the c8-bishop.

3 Nf3 g6? (see diagram)

Now f7 is going to be in serious trouble.

4 Ng5

Moving a piece twice in the opening is often bad, but here it works.

4...Nh6?? (see diagram)

Black has to play 4...e6 or perhaps even 4...Ne5. Now White finishes off things very neatly.

5 Bxf7+! Nxf7 6 Ne6 (see diagram)

A more miserable black queen is hard to imagine. Black's strongest piece is completely powerless.

good to know

Advice on development

Move each of your pieces once. Put it on its best square and leave it there (unless it's attacked).

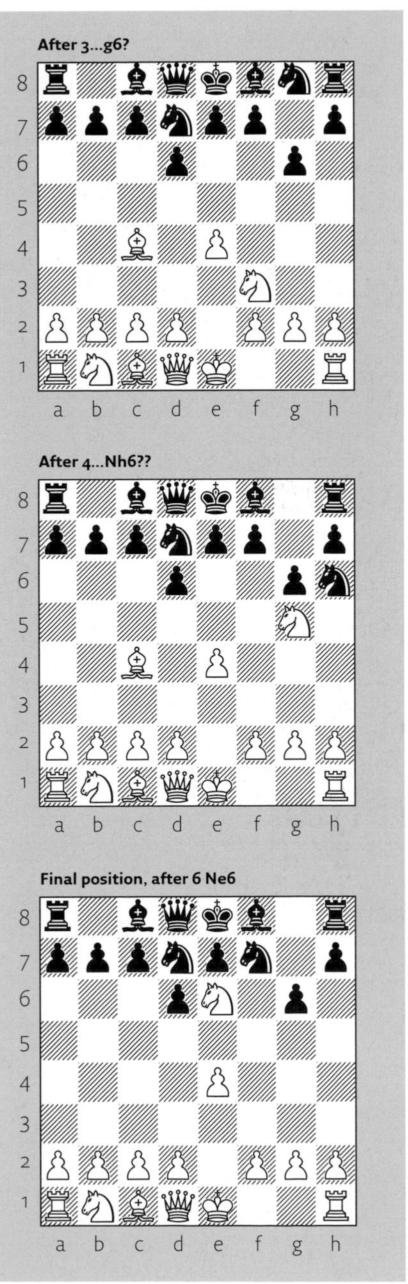

After 3...g6?

After 4...Nh6??

Final position, after 6 Ne6

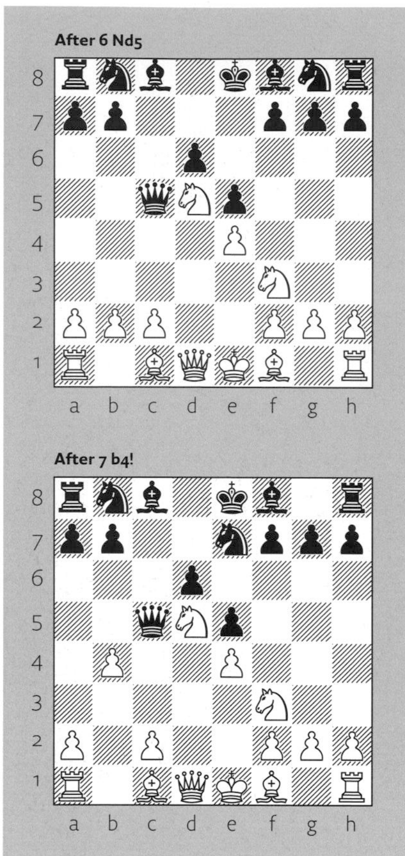

Don't develop your queen too early

Deciding when to develop your queen is a very important decision. If you develop your queen too soon, there is a danger that it will be attacked and even lost.

1 d4 c5 2 dxc5 Qa5+ 3 Nc3 Qxc5

Black has recovered his pawn but his queen is very exposed to attack.

4 e4 e5

Perhaps d6 or Nc6 would have been better. Now White has a very good square for his knight at d5.

5 Nf3 d6

Another move that does not develop a piece.

6 Nd5 (see diagram)

Setting a trap.

6...Ne7

At last a developing move, but a poor one. He doesn't see the trap. 6...Nc6 would allow 7 Nc7+ (fork), winning the a8-rook. 6...Be6 would allow the black queen to retreat to c8 next move.

7 b4! (see diagram)

Out of the blue. It is now clear that the queen has only one square.

7...Qc6 8 Bb5!

Pinning the queen to the king and leaving Black no choice.

8...Qxb5 9 Nc7+

This knight fork wins the black queen.

good to know

Stay at home

Leave your queen at home until you are sure where best to place it.

White develops his queen too early

Here, White is forced to bring his queen into play only to find it has no safe square.

1 d4 Nf6 2 c4 e6 3 Nf3 d5 4 g3

The last move is rather slow – 4 Bg5 or 4 e3 would be better for White.

4...dxc4 5 Nbd2

White could recapture the pawn by 5 Qa4+ and Qxc4 but prefers to delay developing his queen.

5...c5 6 dxc5

This helps Black to develop, but White's d4-pawn was attacked.

6...Bxc5 (see diagram)

Placing the f2-pawn under attack, which White had underestimated.

7 Bg2? Bxf2+! (see diagram)

Black has worked out the rest of the game.

8 Kxf2 Ng4+ 9 Ke1

If White played 9 Kg1 Black would play 9...Qb6+ 10 e3 Qxe3+ 11 Kf1 Qf2 mate. If White tried 9 Kf1 then 9...Ne3+ forks the king and queen.

9...Ne3 10 Qa4+

This is the queen's only safe move.

10...Bd7 (see diagram)

Now, if White plays either 11 Qb4 or 11 Qa3, he will lose his queen when Black responds 11...Nc2+.

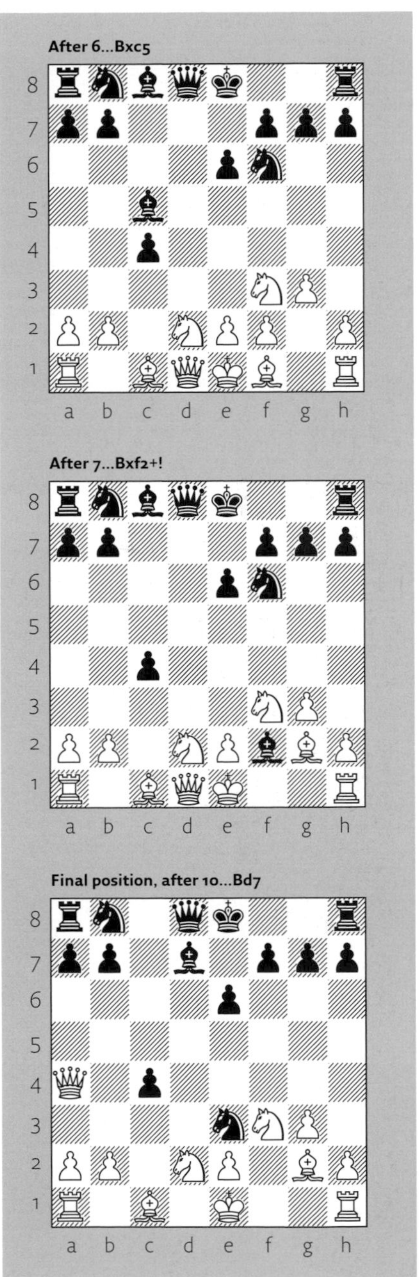

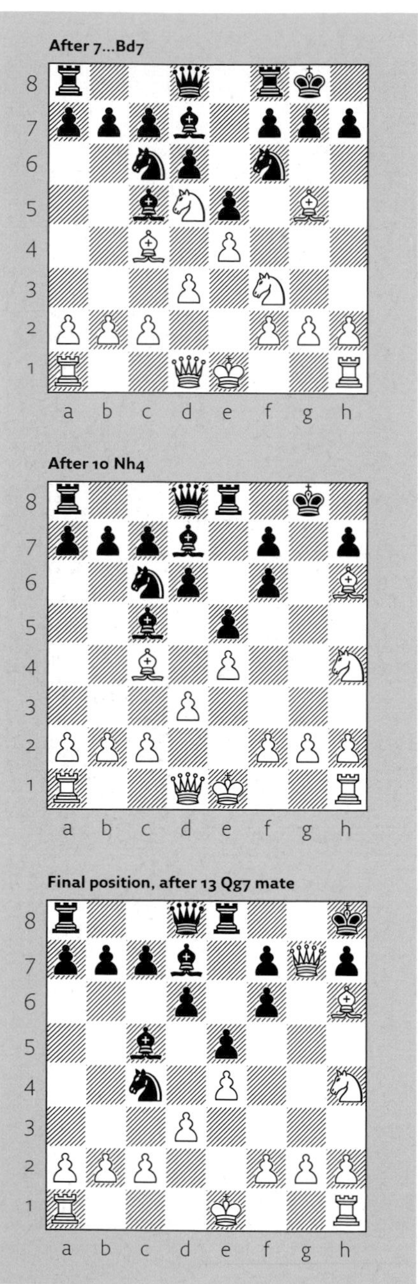

Weakening your opponent's castled position

The three pawns in front of the castled king are an important line of defence. They should be moved as little as possible. If you can force your opponent to weaken these pawns, then your chances of a successful attack have improved.

1 e4 e5 2 Nf3 Nc6 3 Bc4 Bc5 4 Nc3 Nf6 5 d3 0-0

This move is castles, king's side.

6 Bg5 d6 7 Nd5

Now there is nothing Black can do to prevent White from taking on f6 and forcing the reply gxf6, which weakens the king's position.

7...Bd7 (see diagram)

8 Nxf6+ gxf6 9 Bh6 Re8 10 Nh4 (see diagram)

Making it possible for the white queen to join the attack via f3 or h5. This position is very difficult for Black.

10...Na5

Now, if White plays 11 Qh5, attacking f7 a second time, Black can reply 11...Nxc4.

11 Qf3 Nxc4?

Black's only defence was 11...Kh8 (ready to play 12...Rg8), but then 12 Bxf7.

12 Qg3+ Kh8 13 Qg7 mate (see diagram)

Your opponent weakens his own castled position

A little bit of help from your opponent is always welcome.

1 e4 e5 2 Nf3 Nc6 3 Bc4 Bc5 4 Nc3 Nf6 5 d3 d6 6 0-0 Bg4 7 h3 Bh5 8 g4?? (see diagram)

In the previous game White played 7 Nd5 and forced checkmate by taking on f6, exposing the black king. Here White is afraid that this will happen to him if Black is allowed to play Nd4.

8...Nxg4 9 hxg4 Bxg4 (see diagram)

Now Black can choose to play Nd4 or Qf6, both of which attack the pinned knight on f3.

10 Nd5

This stops Qf6 but not Nd4.

10...Nd4 11 Be3

11 Bg5 loses at least a piece after 11...Nxf3+.

11...Nxf3+

Now 12 Kg2 loses the queen after 12...Nh4+, so...

12 Kh1 Qh4+ 13 Kg2 Qh2 mate

(see diagram)

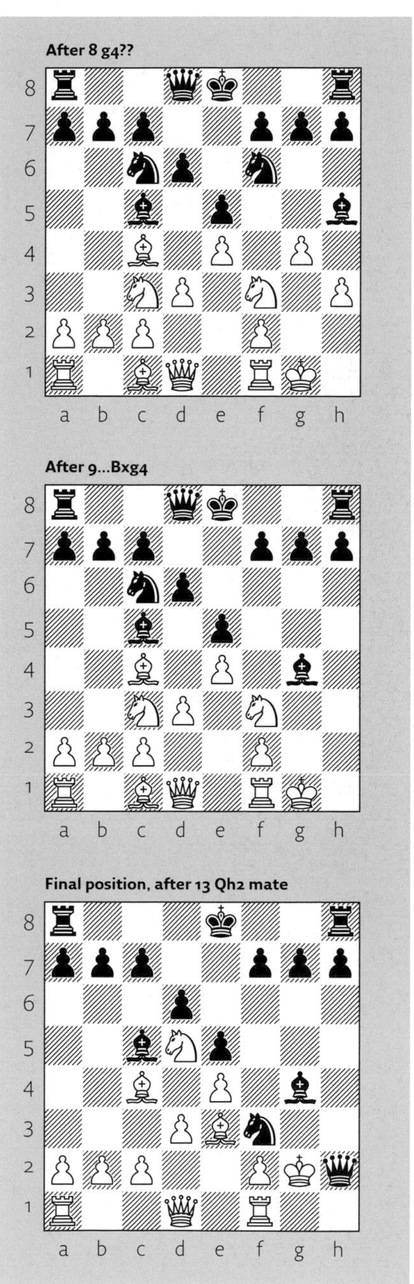

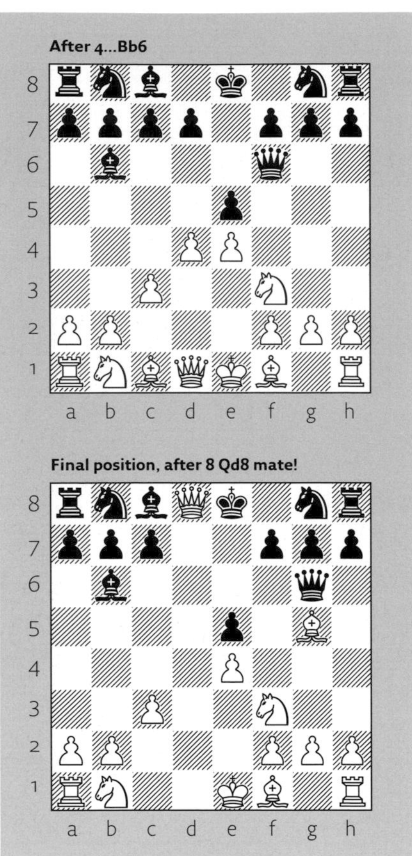

Black develops badly

This game was played nearly 500 years ago between unknown players.

1 e4 e5 2 Nf3

Developing towards the centre.

2...Qf6

This protects the e5-pawn but it is too soon to develop the queen. 2...Nc6 would be a better move.

3 c3

An unnecessary pawn move. 3 Nc3 or Bc4 is simpler. White intends to play d4 as soon as possible.

3...Bc5

A poor developing move as this bishop is going to be attacked by White's d-pawn and so will have to move again.

4 d4 Bb6 (see diagram)

It was important to play 4...exd4 as White can now win a pawn.

5 Be3

White could have taken the e5-pawn.

5...d6

Black is preparing to develop his c8-bishop, but the bad position of his queen is about to become very important.

6 dxe5

Attacking the queen which must not recapture.

6...dxe5 7 Bg5

Again attacking the queen. Now 7...Qd6 is vital.

7...Qg6?? 8 Qd8 mate! (see diagram)

How to develop faster

1 f4

This doesn't help White to develop his pieces.

1...e5

This is a 'gambit'. Black gives away a pawn in order to develop his pieces quickly.

2 fxe5 d6 3 exd6 Bxd6 (see diagram)

Now the idea can be clearly seen. Black has already developed one piece and the others can also appear very quickly. On the other hand, White has made no progress at all and his king is open along the e1/h4 diagonal, which is dangerous.

4 Nc3??

Developing, but a blunder. White should play 4 Nf3 to prevent Black's next move.

4...Qh4+ 5 g3 (see diagram)

White's only move! Black now has two ways to force checkmate. Let's choose the spectacular way.

5...Qxg3+!

The other way to win was by 5...Bxg3+ 6 hxg3 Qxg3 mate, but it's nice to sacrifice your queen.

6 hxg3

Again the only legal move.

7...Bxg3 mate! (see diagram)

This is very similar to Fool's Mate (see page 110).

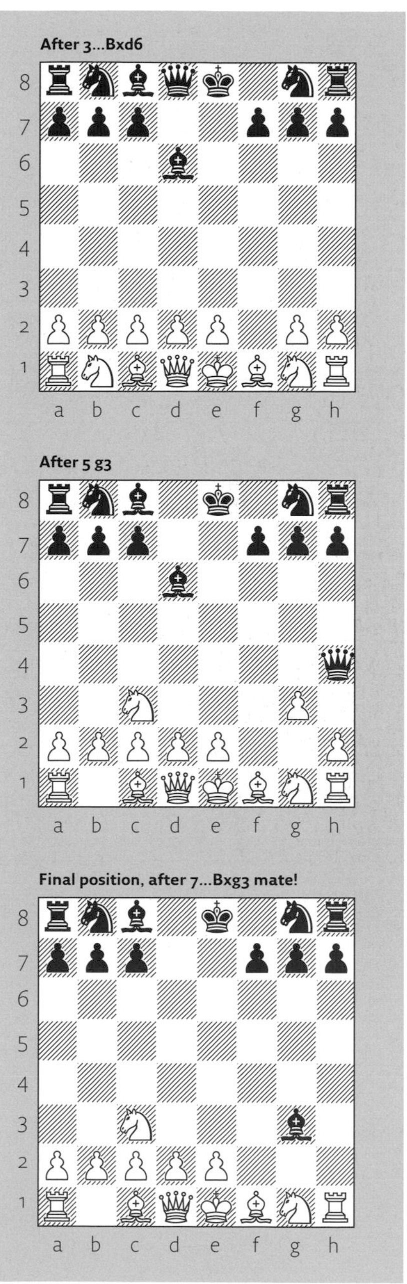

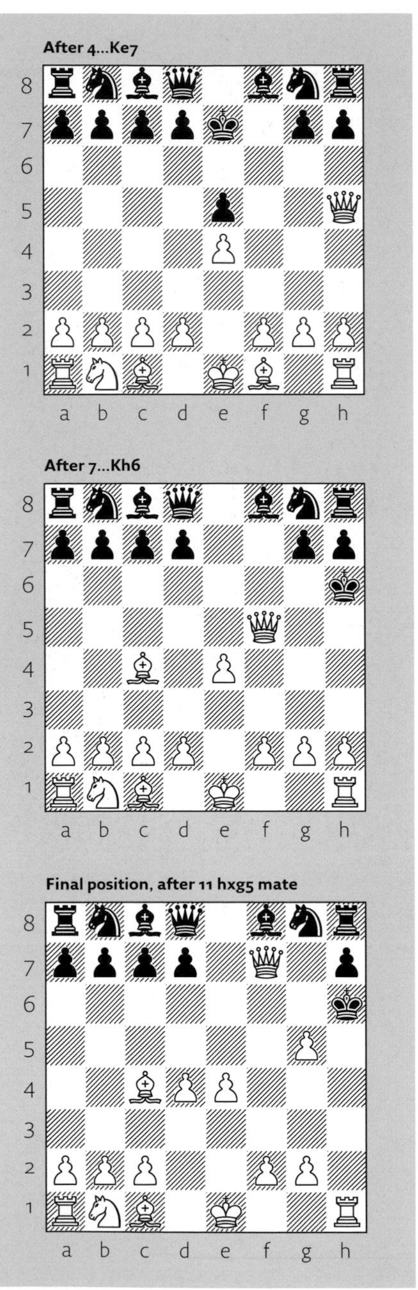

Black exposes his king

1 e4 e5 2 Nf3 f6?

This is not a good move because it does not help Black to develop any pieces and it also opens the h4/e8 diagonal, exposing the black king.

3 Nxe5

White takes immediate advantage.

3...fxe5 4 Qh5+ Ke7 (see diagram)

If Black plays 4...g6 then White continues 5 Qxe5+ and 6 Qxh8.

5 Qxe5+ Kf7 6 Bc4+

Now White has two pieces in his attack.

6...Kg6 7 Qf5+ Kh6 (see diagram)

8 d4+

The c1-bishop joins the attack.

8...g5

The only sensible move.

9 h4

Now the white rook joins in. White is threatening to play 10 hxg5+ Kg7 11 Qf7 mate.

9...Kg7 10 Qf7+ Kh6 11 hxg5 mate (see diagram)

It's double check. White's sacrifice on move 3 is justified because he can play checks on moves 4–8, bringing pieces into his attack. At the end, White isn't so much a piece down as four attacking pieces ahead!

Exploiting f7

The pawns at f2 and f7 are special – they are the weakest on the board. This is because they are only protected by their king. All the other pawns are protected by at least one strong piece.

Anything that is weak is going to be attacked, as we saw in Scholar's Mate (see page 111) and as we see again here.

1 e4 e5 2 Nf3 d6

Black's move blocks the f8-bishop. 2...Nc6 would be a good move, developing a piece.

3 Bc4 Bg4 4 Nc3 g6? (see diagram)

Another move that doesn't help Black's development. 4...Be7 would be better.

5 Nxe5!

Very surprising. If Black takes the knight on e5, then White plays Qxg4 and has won a pawn. But can't Black take the white queen?

5...Bxd1 6 Bxf7+

The weak pawn disappears, leaving Black with only one move.

6...Ke7 7 Nd5 mate! (see diagram)

Of course, White had everything worked out at move 5 or he would not have dared to give away his queen.

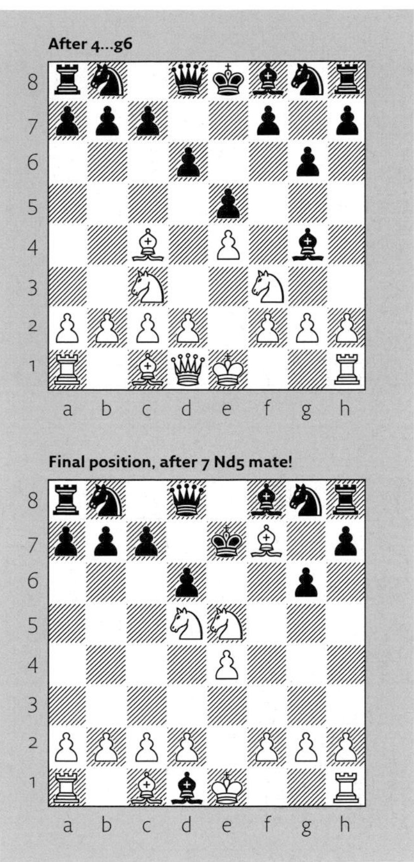

good to know

Targets –f7 and f2

Attacks on f7 and f2 are themes which occur again and again, particularly in the opening. This shows just how sensitive these squares are.

5 Ways to avoid losses

By now you should be aware of some of the main ways in which you can set about winning your opponent's pieces, but what do you do when you get into difficulty yourself? This section includes some tactics and techniques that may get you out of trouble. There is no shortage of ways for you to try to save yourself, but they won't always work!

Unprotected Pieces

We have already seen how important it is to protect your pieces if there is any danger of them being attacked. Any piece that isn't protected could present your opponent with an opportunity.

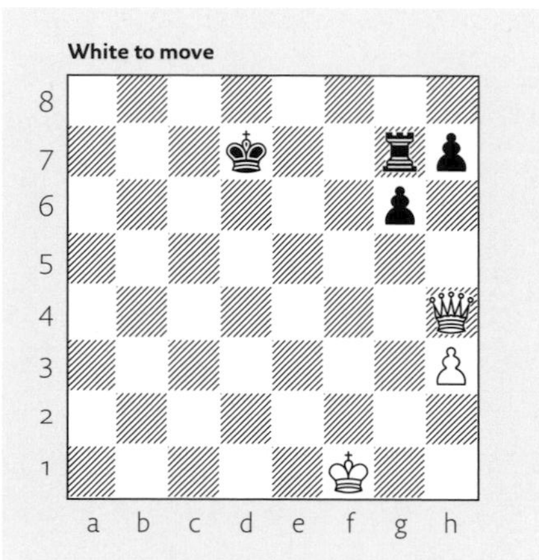

Two simple examples

The rook is unprotected. 1 Qd4+ wins the rook by a queen fork.

The white rook and black king are in line and the black rook is unprotected. 1 Kb6+ is a discovered check that wins the black rook.

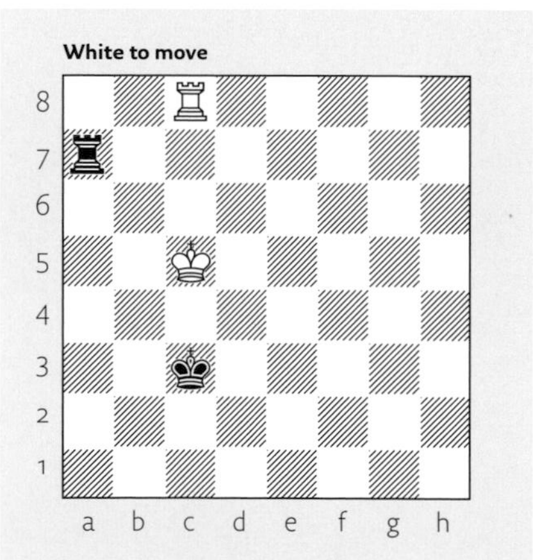

Find the unprotected piece

Which black piece isn't protected?
1 Qa2 wins the rook on g8 which has nowhere safe to go. Black cannot block with the d-pawn because it is pinned.

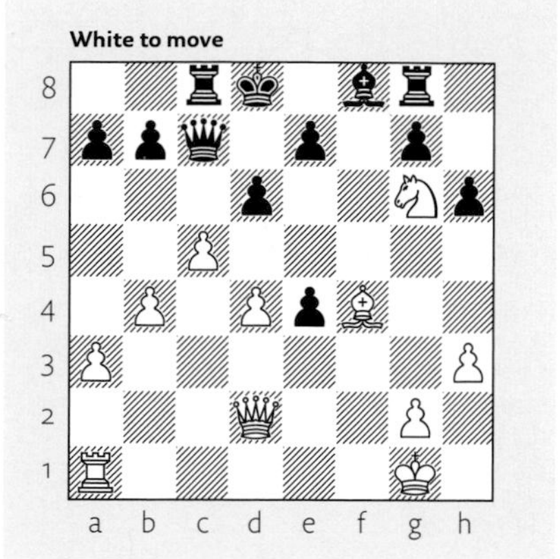

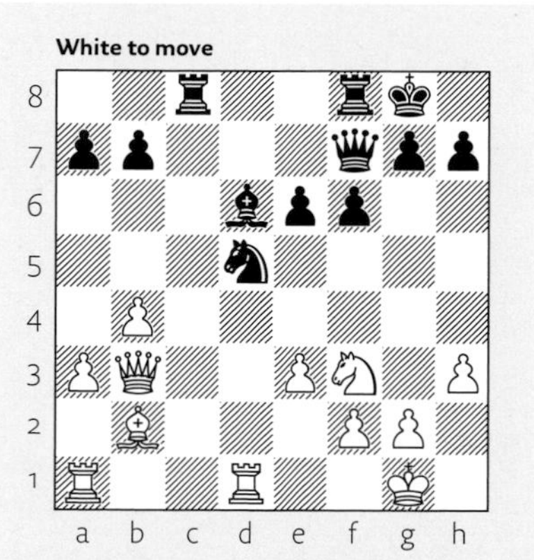

The d6-bishop is unprotected. This means that the d5-knight is pinned – attack it by 1 e4. If the knight stays, then 2 exd5, and if it moves, then 2 Rxd6.

The knight is unprotected. 1 Re8+ Kg7 2 Re7+ is a rook fork that wins the knight.

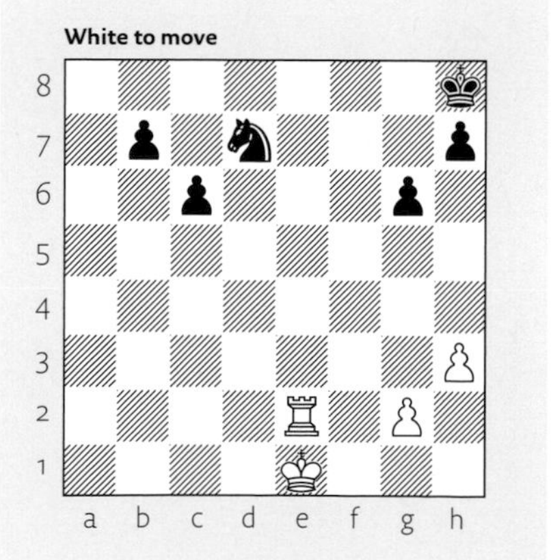

Simple defences

Of course, the best idea is not to get into trouble but, unfortunately, we all find ourselves in difficult situations from time to time. The important thing is not to panic.

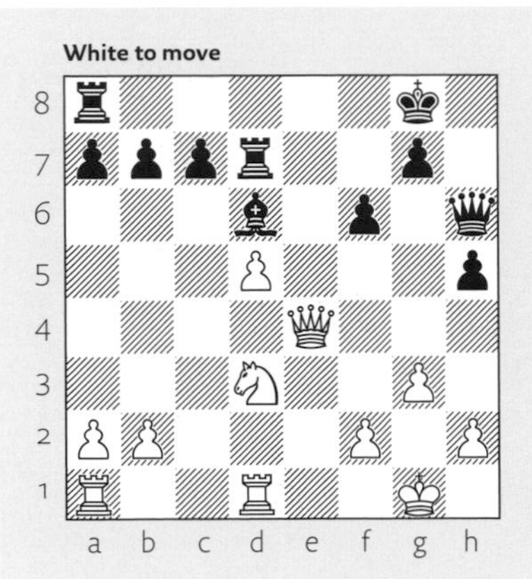

Block the check

White plays the queen fork 1 Qe6+, threatening to win the d7-rook. List the ways to get out of check and try to find one that saves the rook. 1...Rf7 does the trick.

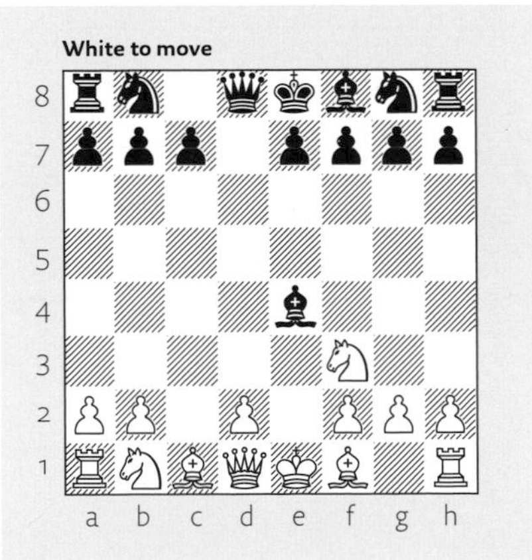

White plays 1 Qa4+ – another queen fork that threatens the undefended bishop on e4. List the ways out of check.

You will find that if Black plays 1...Bc6, he saves the bishop.

Defend with check

If you have two pieces that are being attacked, sometimes you can move one to safety with a check and then, when your opponent has moved out of check, move the other.

Defensive examples

White plays 1 Nc4 and forks the two rooks. 1...Rd1+ isn't possible because of 2 Bxd1, but 1...Ra1+ works – 2 Kh2 and Black moves the d6-rook to safety.

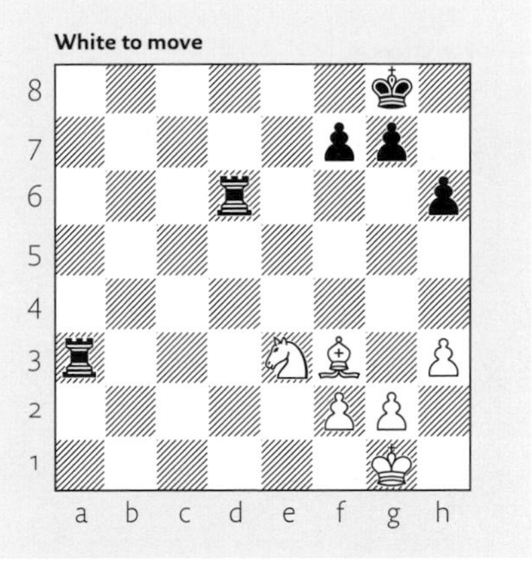

Here, White plays 1 Nxe6 (double attack). White is attacking the rook and threatening the knight fork – 2 Nxf7+. Black plays 1...Rd2+ and then fxe6. The check on f7 is no longer important.

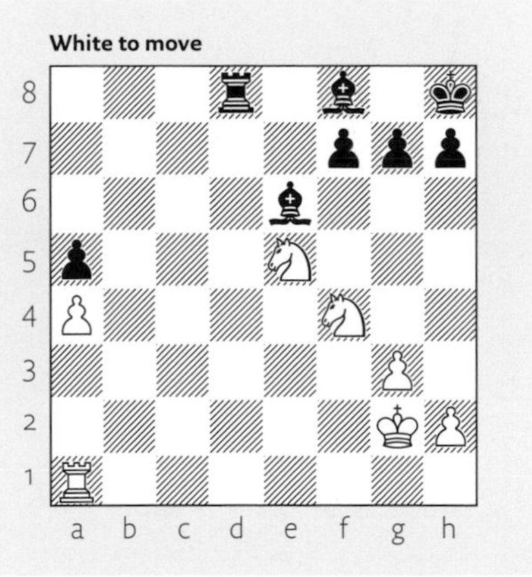

Defend with a mate threat

A move which threatens mate is very powerful and can rarely be ignored. It can get you out of trouble because your opponent has to respond to it instead of carrying on with his own plans.

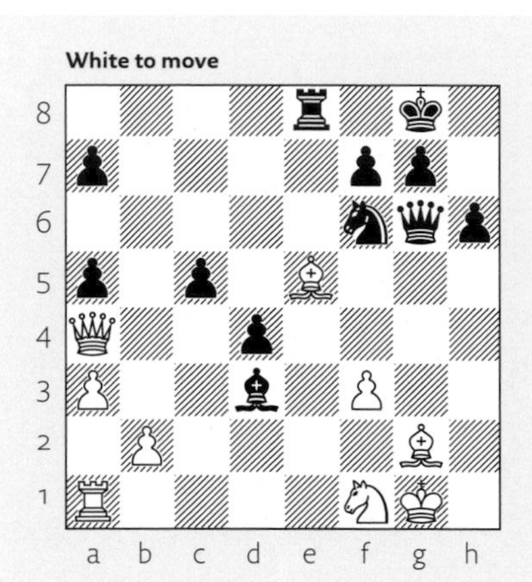

Black threatens mate

In playing 1 Bxf6, White removes the defender of the e8-rook and threatens Qxe8+. Black responds with 1...Re2!, saving the rook and threatening mate by Qxg2.

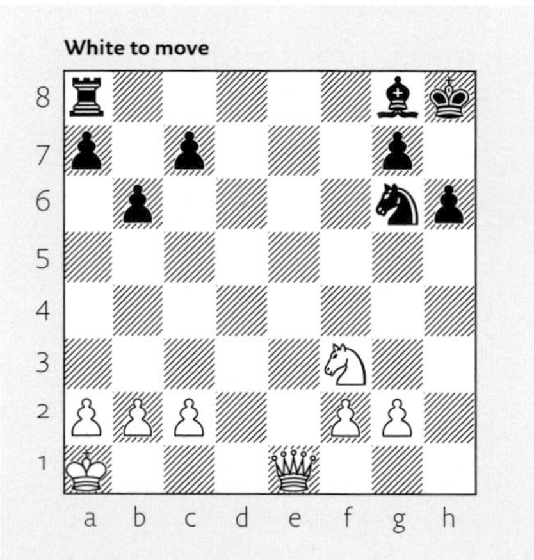

1 Qe4 (queen fork) is answered by 1...Rd8 so that if White plays 2 Qxg6??, Black can play 2...Rd1 mate. White plays 2 b3 and Black saves his knight.

Defend with a pin

You should look for ways to use a pin to prevent losses; not always a pin against the king, it can sometimes be a pin against a major piece or even an undefended minor piece.

Reply with a pin

1 Bd6 (skewer) looks strong. Take advantage of the position of the white queen. 1...Rd8 threatens to win the bishop and forces 2 Bxe7 Rxd2. Black could also avoid loss with 1...Qd8 or 1...Qd7, pinning the white bishop.

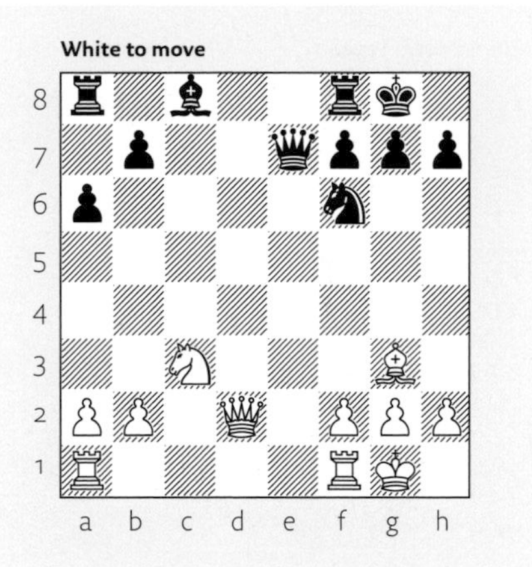

1 Bg5 is an unpleasant fork on the knight and the rook. Black replies 1...Bh6, pinning the white bishop against his king, so White can then only play 2 Bxh6 and Black replies 2...Rxh6.

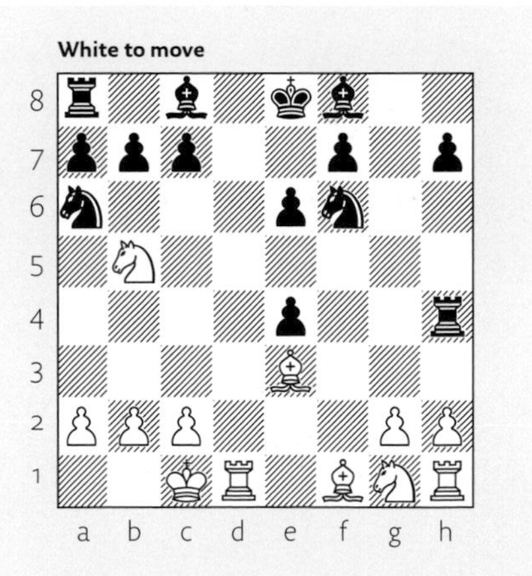

Further defences

Over the next few pages we will see examples of Black using every trick in the book so as to avoid losses, and there are plenty of tricks!

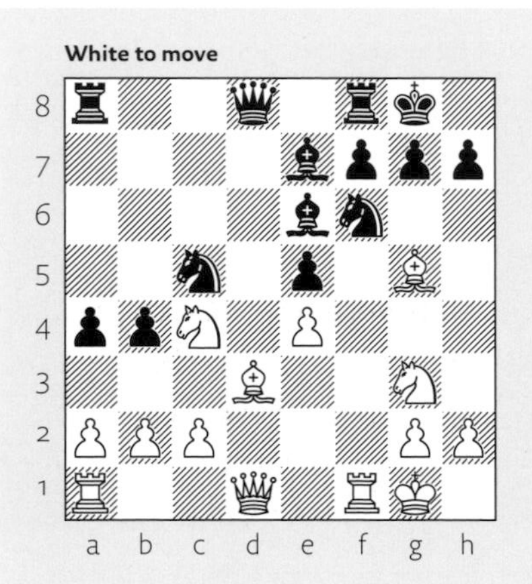

Defend with a fork

The e5-pawn seems to be unprotected, but if 1 Nxe5, then 1...Qd4+ will win the knight.

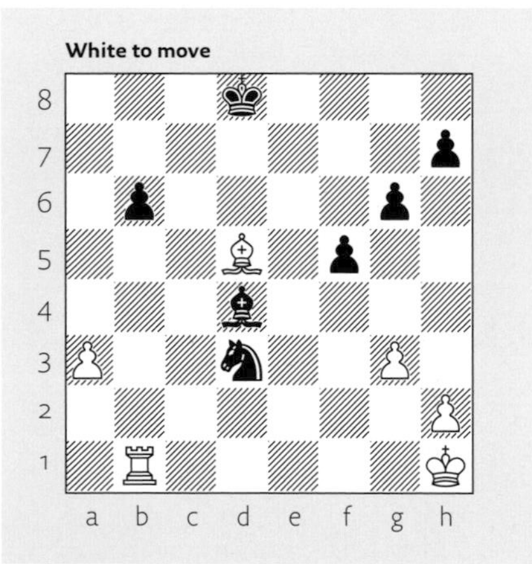

If White plays 1 Rd1 it is a skewer, but also a blunder. Black replies 1...Nf2+ (fork) and wins the rook.

Defend with a skewer

White's move 1 Rxc6 looks good, expecting 1...bxc6 2 Qxc6+ (fork) winning the a8-rook. But Black plays 1...Bd7 (skewer) and can then win the white rook.

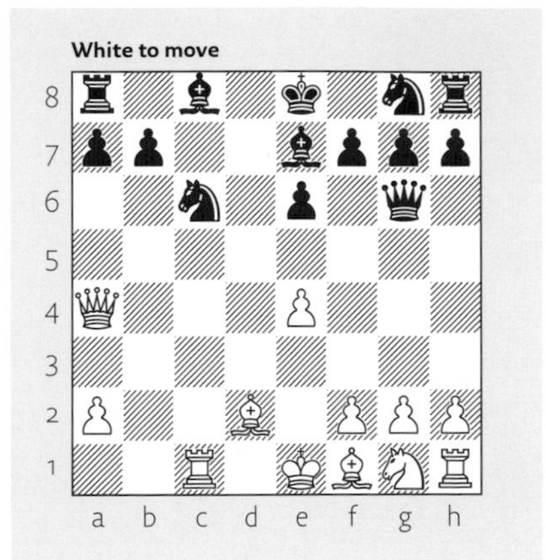

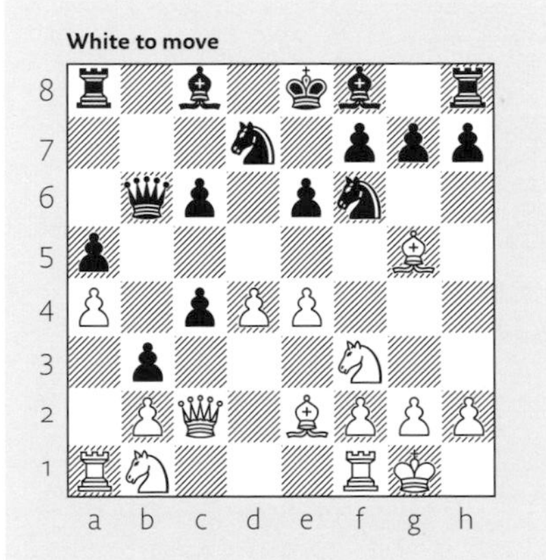

The white queen is under attack from the b3-pawn. If White plays 1 Qxc4, to win a pawn, then 1...Ba6 (skewer) forces 2 Qc1 (the queen's only safe square), 2...Bxe2, winning a bishop.

Counter attack

When you have pieces under attack, look for a move that will threaten one of your opponent's pieces that is as valuable, or more valuable. There are two undefended black pieces, on the fourth rank. 1 Re4 (fork). Black can reply 1...Nc2 (attacking the a1-rook) and after 2 Rc1, Black can play 2...Bf5 saving the bishop and defending the knight.

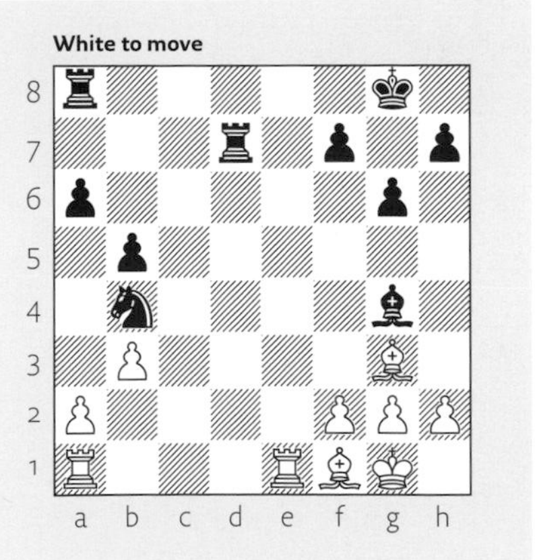

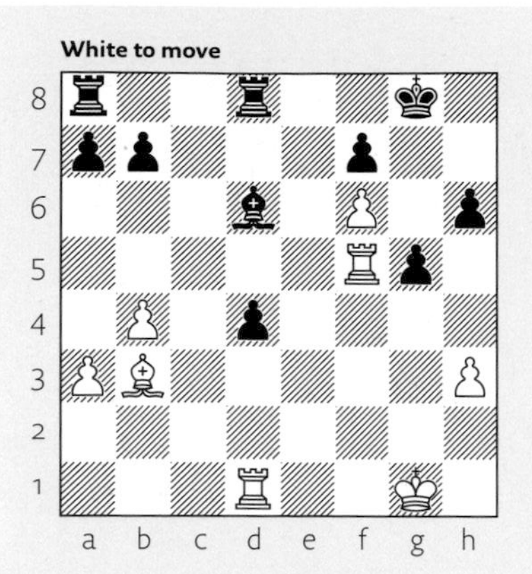

Defend with a double attack

1 Rxd4? The rook on d8 should have warned White that this move is dangerous. Black can play 1...Bh2+ (double attack) 2 Kxh2 Rxd4 or 1...Bc5 (pin) 2 Rxc5 Rxd4.

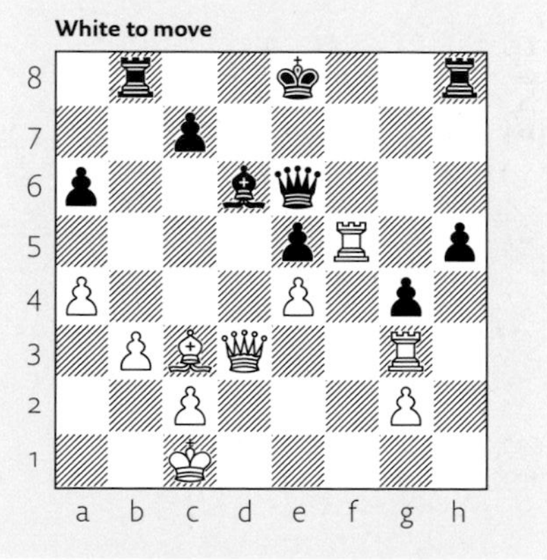

1 Qxa6?? White is about to find out that this pawn is protected. Look for checks. 1...Ba3+ 2 Kb1 Qxa6. Defences along the ranks are hard to spot.

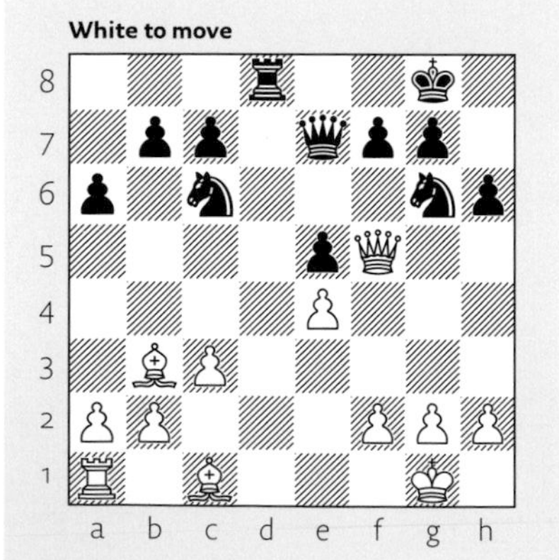

The f7-pawn is pinned, so White tries 1 Qxg6. But White's back rank is weak – 1...Rd1+! 2 Bxd1 (forced) and now the f7-pawn is not pinned, so 2...fxg6.

Defend in other ways

In these two examples, Black gets out of trouble by driving away a defender in order to win a piece.

White's queen is threatened. After 1 Bxc5? Rxa7 2 Bxd6+ Kxd6 White has lost a bishop for a pawn. So instead, White plays just to win a pawn – 1 Qxc5, but is met by 1...Rxh2+! 2 Bxh2 (forced) 2...Qxc5.

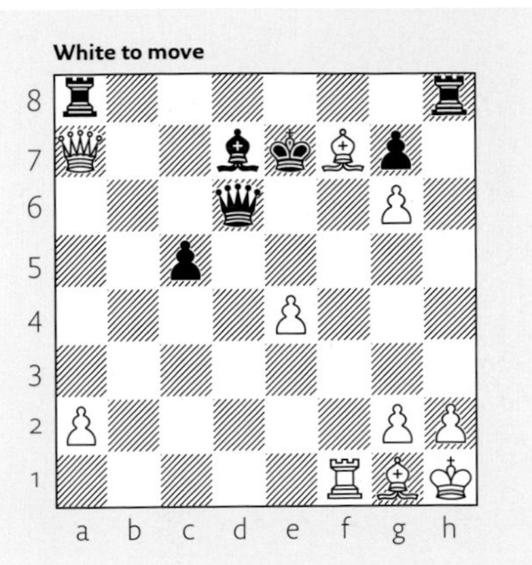

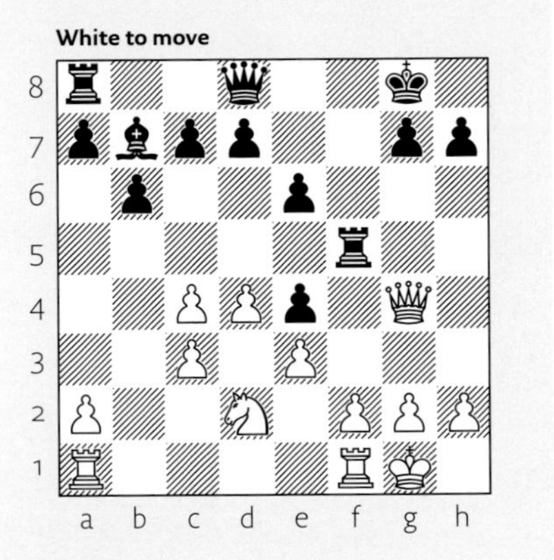

The e4-pawn is attacked twice and is only defended once. 1 Nxe4? After 1...h5, the white queen must move to a square from where it does not defend the knight and allow 2...Bxe4.

must know

Think ahead

Despite these many clever ways to help you get out of trouble, most of the time when you find yourself in difficulties, there is no way out. The best advice is to try to see the problems coming and avoid them.

6 More ideas

You can play chess just for fun or you can play competitively. Those readers who want to go beyond the 'fun' stage will find that chess can be an immensely technical and complicated game, rich in ideas. This chapter will give you the merest glimpse of a few of these ideas, as well as explaining some of the more technical terms that have crept into this book.

Key ideas

The three interlocking ideas of the centre, the development and the initiative underpin all chess games. They are important because of the design of the board and the competitive nature of the game. The other topics here will explain some of the more complex ideas and round off your knowledge of the basics.

good to know

Basic to chess
The fight to control the centre is one of the key themes in most chess openings and is essential in nearly all games. Developing (see page 142) quickly and sensibly is the main way of going about this fight. Seizing and maintaining the initiative is about stamping your authority on the game and making things go your way.

The centre

The importance of the centre is a key idea in chess. By the centre, we mean the four squares in the middle of the board, d4, d5, e4 and e5. There is also a 'central zone' of 16 squares with c3, c6, f3 and f6 at the corners.

We have already seen that most of the pieces become stronger as they get closer to the centre of the board because they attack more squares. But as they come closer to the centre, they also attack more important squares. From the centre they are more likely to create threats and more likely to reduce the scope of the enemy pieces. If you occupy the centre, then not only will your pieces become stronger but your opponents' pieces will probably become weaker.

Remember, your opponent also knows the importance of the centre, so he isn't going to just give it to you. You will have to fight for it!

The battle for the centre often has three stages:

a) establish a pawn in the centre to aid your development
b) increase your control of the centre squares
c) occupy the centre with your pieces.

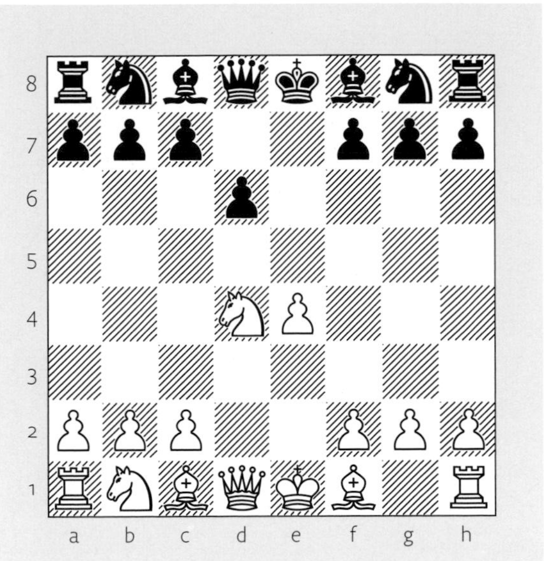

In the opening 1 d4 d5 2 c4, Black usually replies 2...e6 or 2...c6 in order to be able to recapture with a pawn if White should play 3 cxd5. In this way, Black will maintain his pawn centre.

The moves 1 e4 e5 2 Nf3 Nc6 3 c3 are called the Ponziani Opening after an 18th century Italian player/author. The idea is for White to play d4 and to be able to recapture with his c-pawn if Black plays exd4, which would be a mistake because it would leave White with pawns at d4 and e4 and with control of the centre.

After 1 e4 e5 2 Nf3 d6 3 d4 exd4? 4 Nxd4 White's pieces will be able to develop freely, whereas Black's will be obstructed by his d6-pawn. White has more space and the better game.

Development

This is the name given to the process of getting your pieces into play early in the game.

It is of vital importance for you to develop, both in quantity and also in 'quality'. By quality, we mean by putting your pieces on to good squares rather than on to any old square and, as your play and knowledge improve, by placing them so that they work together to pursue a plan.

You have to make pawn moves to get your pieces into play, but every extra pawn move is a piece you haven't developed.

After 1 e4 e5 you can develop your knights or the f1-bishop (not your queen!). It isn't clear where your bishop should go but the knights are almost certain to go to c3 and f3, so develop a knight.

'Knights before bishops' is an old saying.

After 2 Nf3 (attacking the e5-pawn) 2...Nc6 (developing and defending the pawn), you can chose between 3 Bb5 or 3 Bc4. Both are good moves.

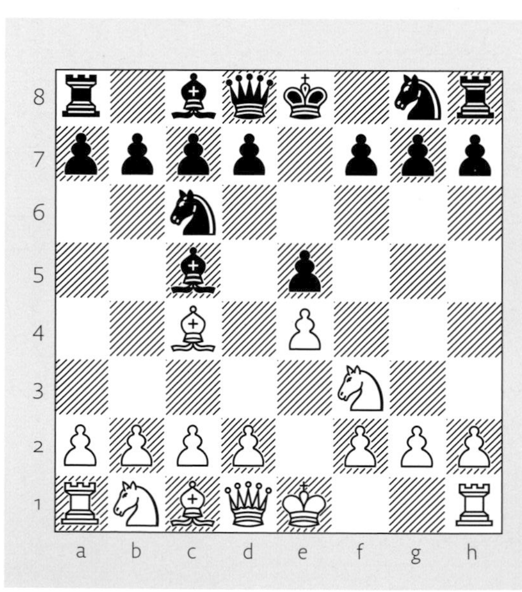

White can also ignore old sayings and play 1 e4 e5 2 Bc4 (aiming at the weak point f7) or 1 e4 e5 2 d4 which also helps his development.

Another old saying is 'move each piece once, put it on its best square and leave it there' (while you develop other pieces).

After 1 e4 e5 2 Nf3 Nc6 3 Bc4 Bc5 look at the possibilities (see diagram).

Here White has several choices:

a) 4 o-o Nf6 5 Nc3 d6 6 d3 and develop quietly, or 4 o-o d6 5 c3 Bg4 6 Qb3 not so quiet at all.

b) 4 Nc3 Nf6 5 d3 is again quiet development; but 5 Nd5 Nxe4 6 Qe2 Nf6 7 d4 is more difficult.

c) 4 d3 Nf6 5 Nc3 d6 6 Bg5 is another quiet way, but Black can choose 4...d6 5 Be3 Bg4.

d) 4 c3 (to attack the centre by d4) 4...Qe7 (to stop d4 because of the possibility of Qxe4+) 5 o-o d6. Can White play 6 d4? Look at his undeveloped queen's side!

e) 4 b4 – White goes on to the attack! He plans 4...Bxb4 5 c3 Bc5 6 d4 attacking the centre and developing quickly. Is it worth a pawn?

Quiet development is sound but easy to defend against. Always look to attack!

good to know

Key ideas

The centre, the development and the initiative are three ideas that are tied together. Between them they tell you to get your pieces out quickly. Do it in a way that helps you to fight for control of the centre. Try to dictate the course of play and develop an attack.

The initiative

Who decides what is happening on the board? Who is dictating the course of the game? The answer is the player with the initiative!

The initiative is the power to make threats that are more powerful than the threats of the opponent. The player with the initiative is the player who is advancing his plans whilst his opponent has to respond rather than advance his own plans.

Because it is usually easier to attack than to defend, having the initiative is very important. That is why some players are happy to give up material to order to obtain, or to keep, the initiative.

But this is also a matter of taste. Some players are happy to take any gifts and to weather the attack with the intention of counter-attacking later. It's a difficult art, but some players specialise in it!

good to know

Still important
The centre, the development and the initiative are also important throughout the game. Once you have developed your pieces, you need to consider how hard they are working. Can you find better squares for them so that they can become more powerful?

At the beginning of the game, White has the initiative because he has the first move. His job is to keep it and to try to build on it. Black's job is to try to cancel it out (to 'equalise') and then to assume the initiative himself.

Your initiative is growing if:

a) your lead in development is growing

b) your opponent's king gets into difficulties

c) you saddle your opponent with a weakness – a backward pawn, an isolated pawn, a bad bishop

d) you increase your control of the centre

e) you increase the power of your pieces.

If you win material and keep the initiative, you should have a won position.

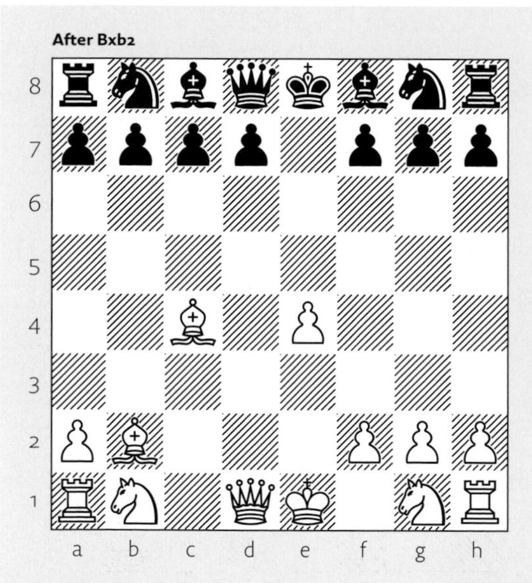

Some of the most interesting, and difficult, questions in chess arise when one side gives up material in order to increase their initiative into an outright attack. After the moves 1 e4 e5 2 d4 exd4 3 c3 dxc3 4 Bc4 cxb2 5 Bxb2 White has a wonderful attacking position, but is it worth two pawns?

Black has done nothing wrong so he should be able to equalise.

Gambits

In some chess openings, one side gives up material in order to gain time for the development of pieces. Such openings are called 'gambits'.

Here are some examples:

Queen's Gambit Accepted: 1 d4 d5 2 c4 dxc4

Queen's Gambit Declined: 1 d4 d5 2 c4 e6 (or 2...c6)

Albin Counter Gambit (Albin was a late nineteenth century player): 1 d4 d5 2 c4 e5

King's Gambit Accepted: 1 e4 e5 2 f4 exf4

King's Gambit Declined: 1 e4 e5 2 f4 Bc5 (or other second moves)

Falkbeer Counter Gambit (Falkbeer was a famous nineteenth century player): 1 e4 e5 2 f4 d5

From's Gambit (From was a nineteenth century Danish player): 1 f4 e5 2 fxe5 d6 3 exd6 Bxd6. It is easy to see in this position that Black will be able to develop his pieces much faster than White.

Open file/half-open file

An open file is one without pawns. On a half-open file only one side has a pawn.

Open file

The c-file is open and White controls it and has a big advantage. If both sides have rooks on an open file, then there are usually exchanges.

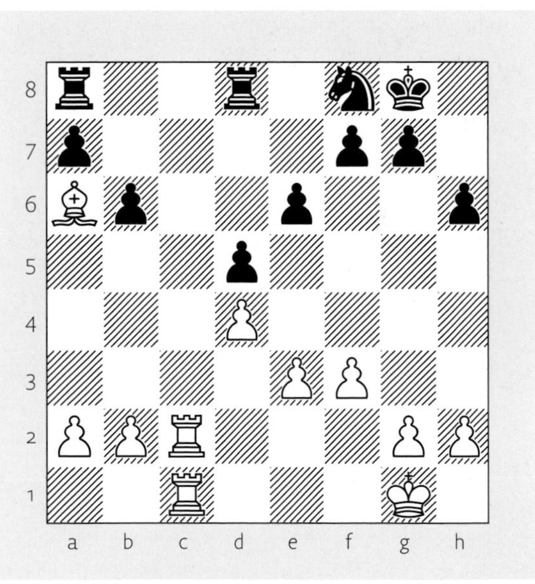

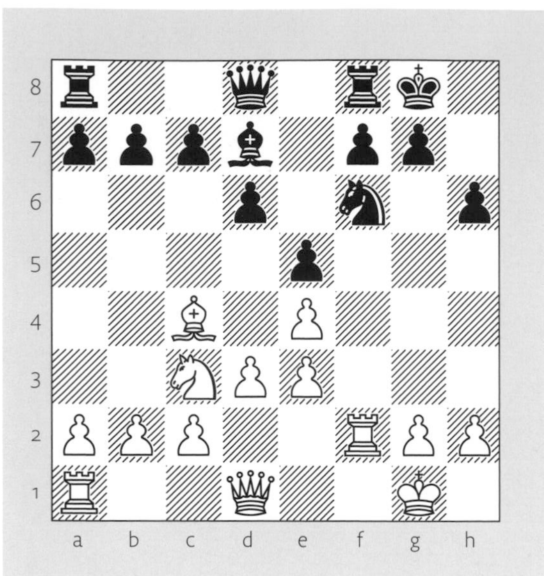

Half-open file

The f-file is half-open. This means additional power for the white rooks.

White will probably play his queen and play Raf1.

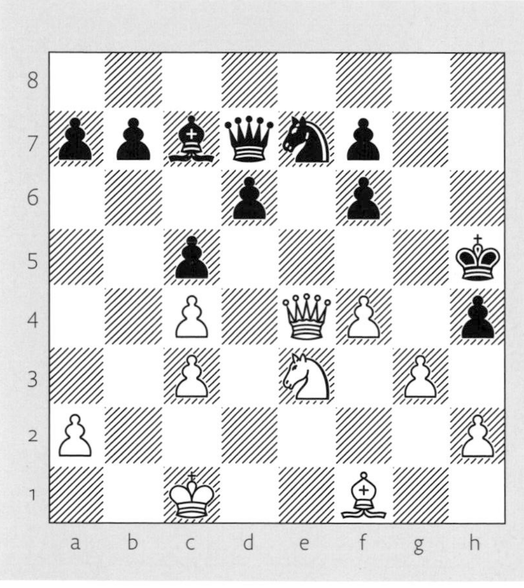

Sacrifice

Deliberately giving up material in order to win back more material later or to get an important advantage in position, is called 'making a sacrifice'.

White sacrifices his queen at the right moment: **1 Be2+** (Black has only one reply) **1...Kh6** (the black king is now on the right square for a knight fork) **2 Qxe7!** (Black must recapture or he will be a piece down) **2...Qxe7 3 Nf5+** (and White will regain his queen with an easily won position.

The Exchange

'The Exchange' is the difference between a rook and a knight or a rook and a bishop. A player who wins a rook for a knight (or bishop) is said to have 'won the exchange'.

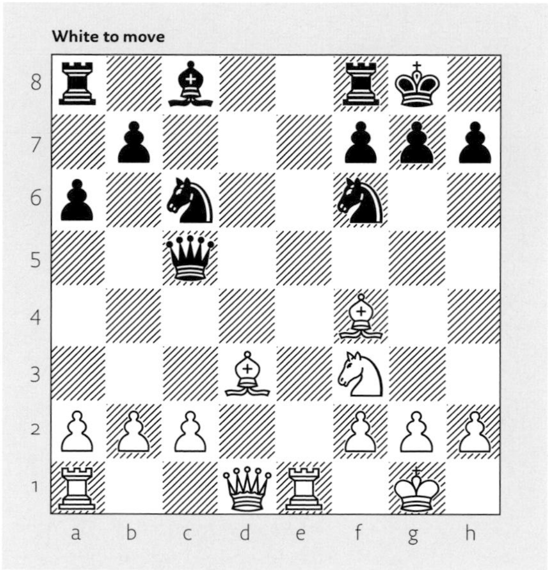

1 Bd6 forks the black queen and f8-rook and 'wins the exchange' after Black moves his queen and White plays **2 Bxf8 Kxf8**. Black must not play 1...Qxd6 because of 2 Bxh7+ Kxh7 3 Qxd6 and Black has lost his queen.

did you know?

Blunder

A blunder is a mistake so serious that the player who has made it will lose the game (or perhaps turn a win into a draw) if his opponent replies correctly.

must know

Combination

The name given to a series of moves linked by an idea is a 'combination'. This usually involves some forcing moves – captures, checks, mate threats or other threats. See the example under Sacrifice on the opposite page.

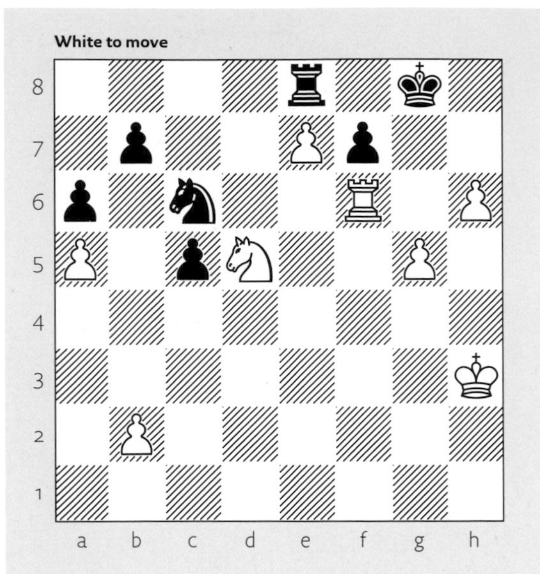

Passed pawn

A pawn which doesn't have an enemy pawn in front of it or on an adjoining file is a 'passed pawn'.

White's pawns at e7 and h6 are passed pawns and very dangerous. **1 Rxc6** (vacating f6 for his knight) **1...bxc6 2 Nf6+ Kh8 3 Nxe8** and the e-pawn will promote.

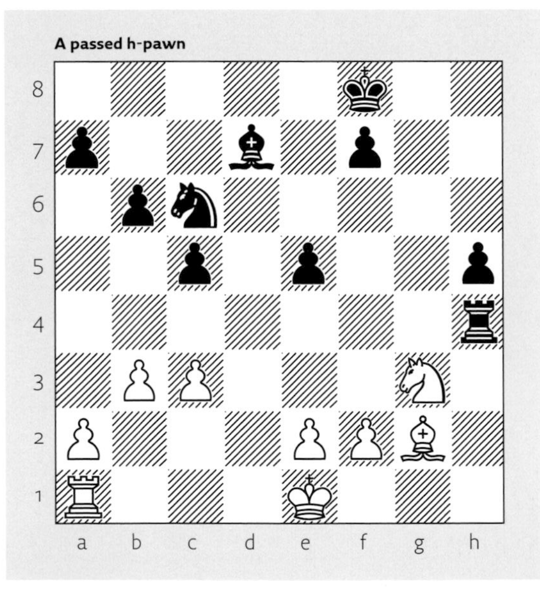

The h-pawn is a passed pawn. It has potential but isn't dangerous yet. Black would prefer to have his rook behind the pawn so that it supports the pawn as it advances. Black's problem is that if he moves the rook, White may be able to play Nxh5.

Isolated pawn

An isolated pawn is one which doesn't have a pawn which can protect it.

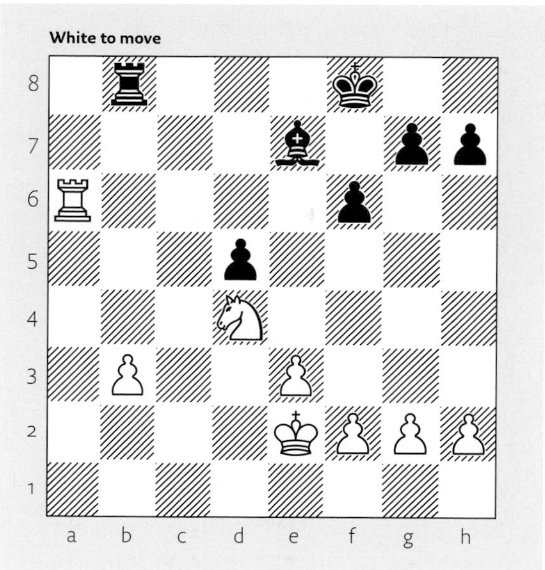

White's b-pawn and Black's d-pawn are both isolated pawns. These are usually weaknesses because they have to be protected by a piece, which is not a good way to use your forces.

White could attack the d-pawn from a5 or by playing Ra7 and Rd7.

Doubled pawns

Two pawns on the same file are 'doubled pawns'. They might be a weakness if they make it harder to create a passed pawn in an ending. On the other hand they can be a strength because they guarantee an open (or half-open) file – for the rooks.

did you know?

Pawn problems

Because pawns are less mobile than the other pieces and cannot move backwards, they often become weaknesses and have to be defended by stronger pieces. This is a wasteful use of the stronger pieces, so the pawns must be used with great care to avoid them becoming weak.

good to know

Under promotion
On the rare occasions when a pawn promotes to something other than a queen, it is said to under promote. This can happen so as to avoid stalemate or, if promoting to a knight, to give check.

Backward pawn

A pawn behind other pawns, of the same colour, on adjoining files, is said to be 'backward'. It is generally weak because it has to be defended by a piece. If it is on a half-open file then it is even weaker. The best remedy is to advance the pawn or to try to exchange it, perhaps both.

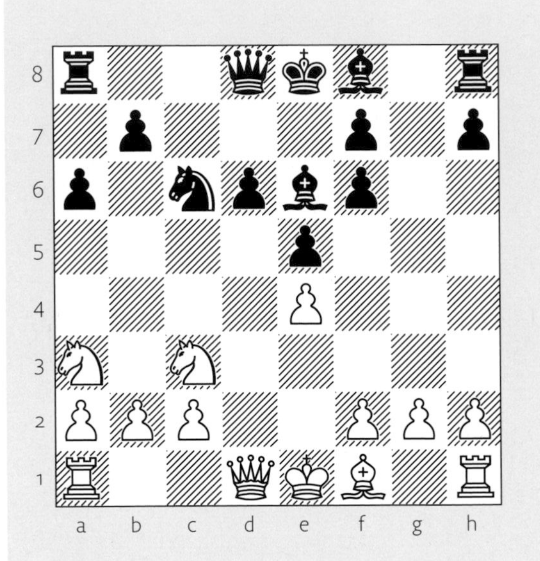

Black has two backward pawns at d6 and f6 (which is also a doubled pawn). The d6-pawn is especially weak because White has no d-pawn and so is likely to attack down the d-file. If you move White's knight from a3 to e3, he would have control of the d5 and f5 squares, giving Black serious trouble.

In the diagram, from a World Championship match, Black played **11...d5** and after **12 exd5 Bxa3 13 bxa3 Qa5 14 Qd2 0-0-0** (castles queen's side – pinning the pawn!) his position was okay.

United passed pawns

Two (or more) passed pawns on adjoining ranks are called 'united passed pawns'. Such pawns are frightening things, when properly supported. Enemy pieces cannot easily stand in front of them because, as the pawns advance, they push everything out of their way. The further advanced they are, the stronger they become until, by the time they reach the sixth (or third) rank, combinations become possible to force them through to promotion.

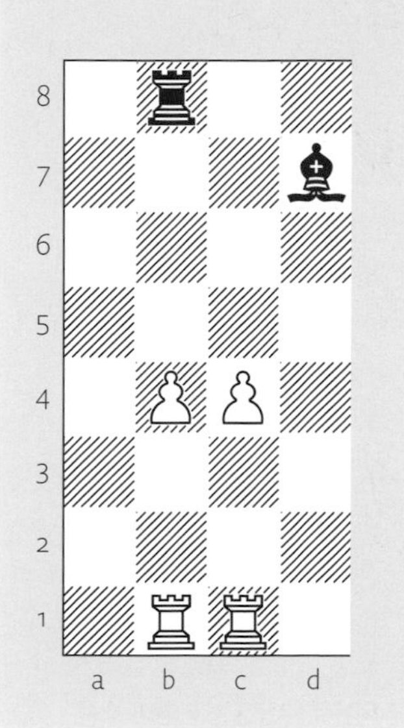

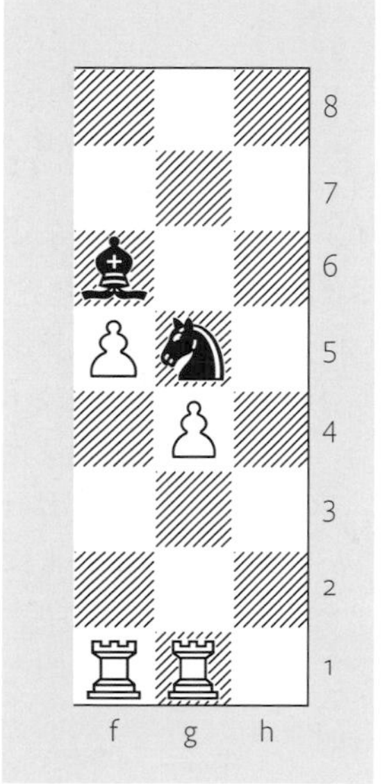

On files b and c are well-supported passed pawns which cannot be approached by the enemy – very strong. On files f and g is another pair showing them at their weakest. Even then they are still strong because it takes 2 pieces to stop them. White will try to exchange the black pieces and advance the pawns. Black will try to attack the backward g-pawn or create play somewhere else on the board.

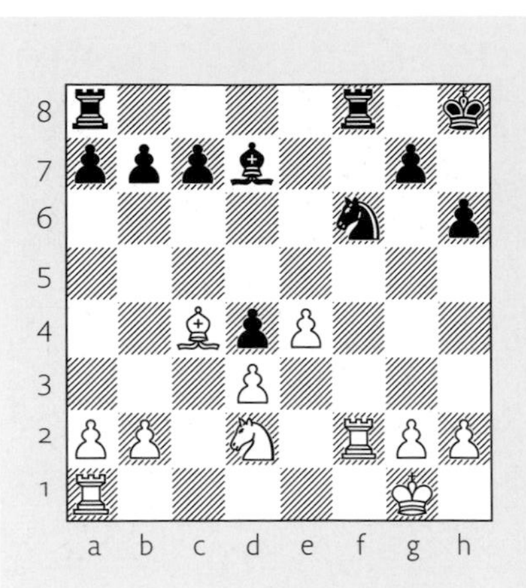

Protected passed pawn

A passed pawn which is protected by another pawn is known as a 'protected passed pawn'.

It is a long term asset whose strength will normally only be apparent in the endgame. In this position White would like to exchange rooks on the f-file, advance his king into the centre and eventually push the passed e-pawn.

The existence of the passed pawn will serve to restrict the movement of Black's pieces.

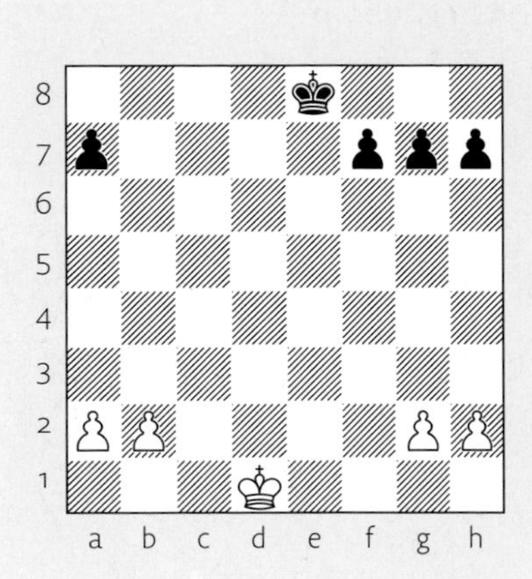

Pawn majority

The diagram shows each side with a pawn majority – more pawns than your opponent in one area of the board.

The importance of a pawn majority is that you can create a passed pawn, if you play the pawns correctly.

White has two pawns to one on the queen's side while Black has 3 against two on the king's side. White should be able to create a passed pawn quicker than Black because he has fewer pawns to advance and that takes fewer moves.

The general rule is to advance the pawn which doesn't have another pawn on its file. See the example on page 104.

Doubled rooks

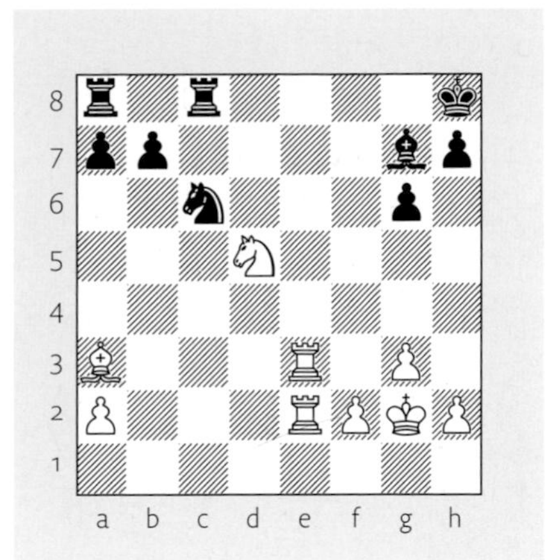

Open files are natural places to put rooks. Straight line pieces are often blocked by other pieces, so it is natural to place a rook on an open file, to increase the power of the rook. By placing both rooks on an open file (doubling rooks) further power for the rooks is secured.

Both sides have powerful bishops and White's knight is very well placed for the attack. The main difference between the sides lies in the rooks. White's are doubled and threatening to penetrate the black position, whilst Black's rooks are passive and one is undeveloped. White needs to use his control of the e-file to advance his rook to e7 but he must be careful. **1 Ne7 Nxe7 2 Rxe7** (if 2...Bf8 – skewer – 3 Bb2+ Kg8 4 Rxb7).

Rook on the 7th (2nd) rank

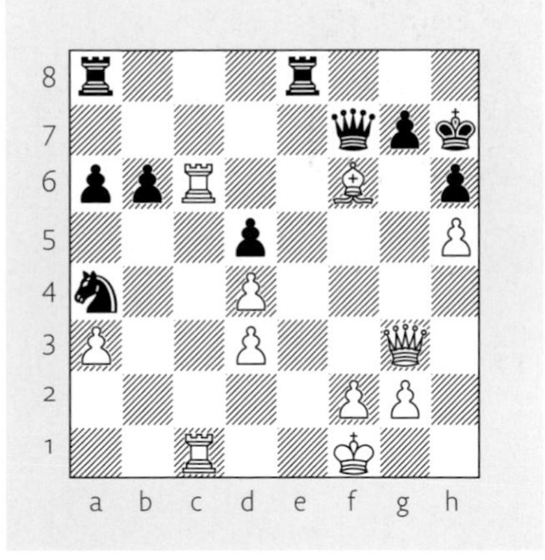

To maximise the power of your rooks, you need to help them to operate along ranks as well as files. Your opponent's second rank is usually full of his pieces, so that's a good place for your rook. So, Step 1 is to put your rooks on an open file; Step 2 is to advance a rook to the 7th (2nd) rank. The alternative is to go for your opponent's back rank and to attack his pawns from behind.

White controls the c-file and can easily play Rc7 (protected by his queen as well as his rook). The black queen and king are both on the 7th rank. White's problem is that his bishop is threatened. **1 Bxg7! Qxg7 2 Rc7** (pin) **2...Re7 3 Rxe7** (pin!) **3...Qxe7 4 Rc7** (pin) wins the queen.

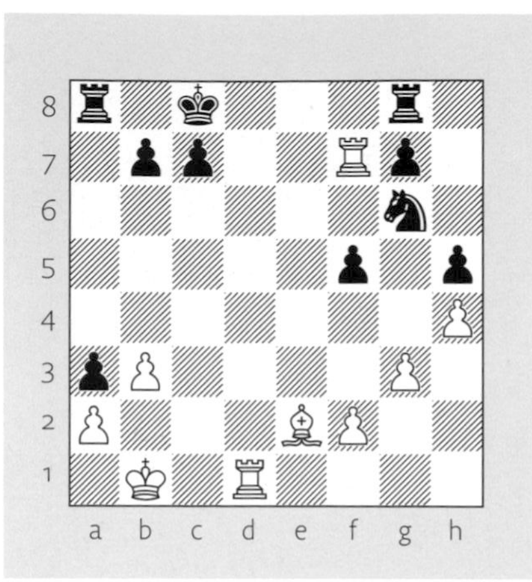

Doubled rooks on the 7th (2nd)

When one side has both rooks on his opponent's 2nd rank, he has a ferocious attack, strong enough to make most players resigned to their fate. This is especially true if the defending king is trapped on its back rank.

Instead of just grabbing one of the available black pawns, White plays **1 Rdd7** after which everything on the Black second rank is under threat as well as the f5 and h5 pawns. If Black plays 1...Ne5, White get out of the fork by 2 Rxc7+.

Opposite coloured bishops

When each side has only one bishop and they move on different coloured squares, they are said to have 'opposite coloured bishops'. In the middle game, this helps the attacking side as the defender finds it hard to compete on the squares controlled by the attacker's bishop. In the ending, opposite coloured bishops make a draw more likely, especially if they are the only pieces left. This is because the defending bishop can blockade a passed pawn and it is difficult to force it away.

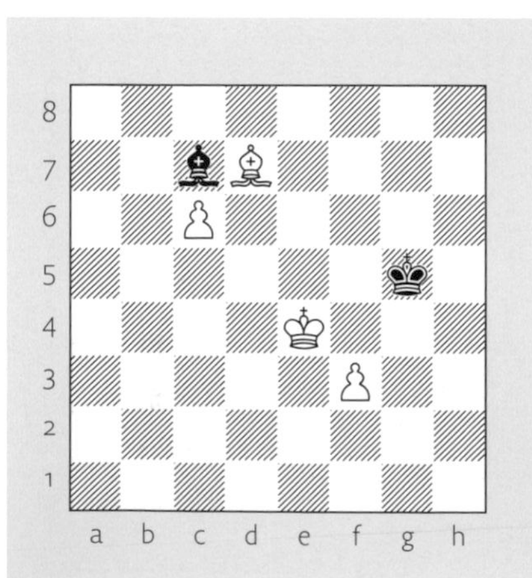

White is two pawns ahead but he cannot win because he cannot queen either pawn. Black has only to move his bishop along the h2/b8 diagonal to prevent the pawns from advancing. If the white king goes to b7, then the black king moves to prevent the advance c6-c7.

Bad bishop

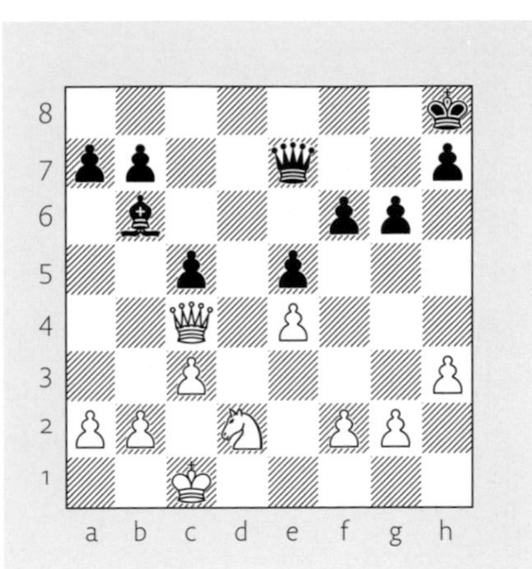

A bad bishop is one that is restricted by its own pawns because they stand on squares of the same colour as itself. Even worse, when the pawns of the two sides are locked together, then the opponent's pawns will be on the other colour and the bishop will not be able to attack them.

If you have a bad bishop, or one that is likely to become bad, then try to exchange it or, failing that, try to get it outside its own pawns when it will have more scope.

Black has a bad bishop because of the pawns on c5, e5 and f6. White's knight is a much better piece especially if White can manoeuvre it to d5.

Back rank mate

This is one of the commonest checkmates. Here are four typical ways in which it occurs.

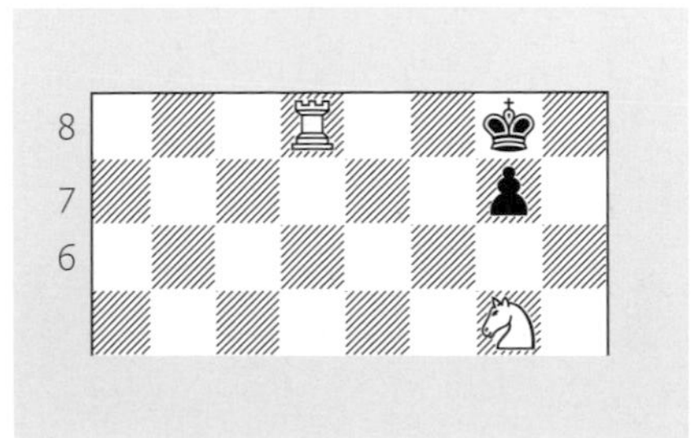

good to know

More examples
If you want to see how a Smothered Mate can come about in a game, then have a look at page 114.

On page 117 you will find a similar idea where the queen is the victim.

Smothered Mate

This is the name given to a very specific checkmate. We have already seen some Smothered Mates from a knight where the defending king is surrounded by his own pieces. There is a famous Smothered Mate which is similar but more attractive because it ends with a sacrifice.

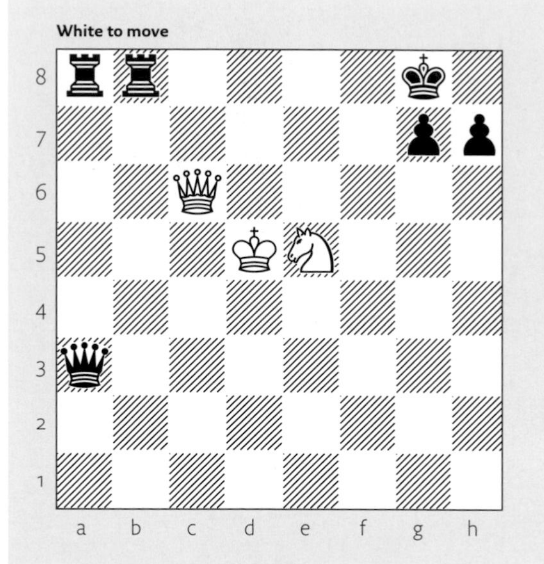

This mate is sometimes called 'Philidor's Legacy' but this position is from 1497! That's more than 200 years before Philidor was born (see page 160).

White forces mate by **1 Qe6+ Kh8** (if 1...Kf8 then 2 Qf7 mate) **2 Nf7+ Kg8** (setting up a discovered check) **3 Nh6+** (double check!) **3...Kh8** (again if 3...Kf8 then 4 Qf7 mate) **4 Qg8+!! Rxg8 5 Nf7 mate!**

This is very rarely seen but it does occur from time to time as a threat and has to be avoided.

Perpetual check

One of the ways in which a game can be drawn is if one player achieves a position in which he can keep checking. This will usually only happen if the checking player is in danger of losing and a draw is the preferable alternative.

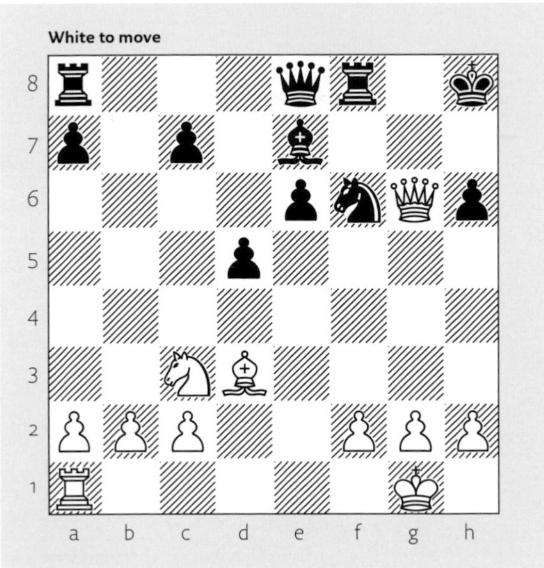

White is a rook to a pawn down and so plays for the draw. **1 Qxh6+ Kg8 2 Qg5+ Kh8 3 Qh6+** and so on (forever). It's a draw.

Repetition of moves

This is yet another way of drawing a game. If the same position occurs 3 times, with the same player to move each time, then the player about to move and repeat the position, may claim a draw. This really only applies to games in competition.

good to know

Another way to draw
What happens if you exchange so many pieces that there isn't enough material left on the board to force mate? It isn't possible to mate with a king and a knight or a king and a bishop, or even with a king and two knights. You might have a king and a pawn against a lone king, but not be able to promote the pawn.

In all of the above circumstances, the game is a draw. If you can't mate. you can't win.

7 Leading players

The names of a few early leading players, and some examples of their skill, have come down to us through their books. This thin trickle of information increased enormously in the 1830s when chess magazines began to appear, and by 1886 we had the first match for the World Chess Championship. The World Chess Federation (FIDE) was formed in 1924 and this organisation arranged the World Team Championship and Women's World Championship from 1927. It is now also responsible for the (men's) World Championship.

Best players and champions

The top players of the early 19th century are sometimes referred to as World Champions, but in those days no-one thought in such terms. In fact, the first World Championship was in 1886.

did you know?

Chess moves
Spain was the first top country for modern chess. Superiority then moved to Italy and afterwards to France. By the mid-19th century, England was the centre of chess and then Germany. By the 1930s, the USA was carrying all before it and after 1945, Soviet Russia became top dog.

Ruy Lopez de Segura

The most famous early chess player lived in Spain from about 1530 until 1580. His name was Ruy Lopez de Segura and we know of him because he wrote a book on the game. He played chess at the court of the King of Spain and was one of the leading players of his time.

François-André Danican Philidor (1726–95)

Philidor was probably the best chess player of the 18th century. He wrote a famous book on the game that appeared in several languages and many editions. About 70 of his games have survived, but all from late in his life.

Philidor came from a well-known family of musicians and chess players who were part of the French royal court. He was a composer who specialised in comic opera. He learned to play chess at the age of about 14 and quickly became one of the best players in Paris.

During the last 25 years of his life, he made over 20 trips to London, often staying for several months at a time, and earned his living by giving chess lessons and playing games for wagers.

His ability to play two games at once without seeing the board (so-called 'blindfold chess') was greeted with awe.

Howard Staunton (1810–74)

The Englishman, Howard Staunton, became a leading player in about 1840. In 1843, he beat the Frenchman, Pierre St-Amant (1800–72), and for a few years Staunton was the strongest player in the world.

He was the editor of several chess magazines, a famous chess column in the *Illustrated London News* and he helped to organise the first international tournament in London in 1851. There he lost to the German, Anderssen (see page 162), and finished only fourth.

The design of chess pieces used today are known as the Staunton Pattern and have become the standard. Other designs were too ornate and impractical for regular play. The editor of a well-known edition of Shakespeare, Staunton was widely admired but equally widely disliked. Many hundreds of his games survive.

ABOVE: Howard Staunton, the world's best player in the 1840s.

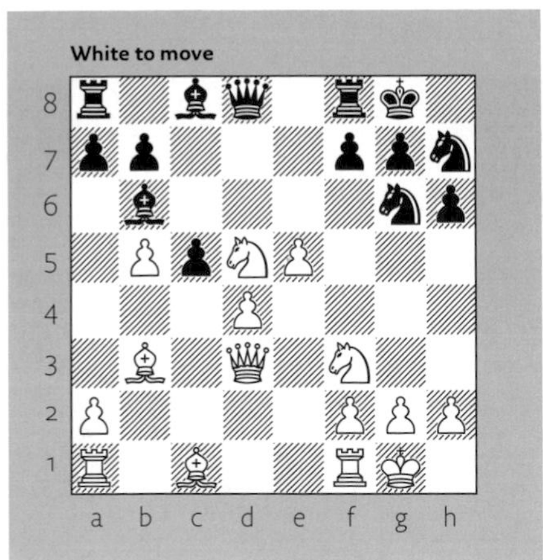

White: H. Staunton
Black: an unknown player

(see diagram)

Black probably should have played 14...Be6. **15 Qxg6!!** This wonderful sacrifice sets up a double check. **15...fxg6 16 Ne7+** The king must move. **16...Kh8 17 Nxg6 mate.**

ABOVE: Adolf Anderssen, mathematics teacher and attacking genius.

Adolf Anderssen (1819–79)

Anderssen was recognised as the world's leading player after he won an international chess tournament in London in 1851. He was a mathematics teacher from Breslau (now Wroclaw, Poland, but then in Germany). He was a quiet, shy man who dominated German chess in Berlin and Leipzig with his brilliant attacking play.

He lost a match against Paul Morphy (see opposite), a player on a different level altogether, but after Morphy's retirement from play, Anderssen again became the leading practising player.

White: A. Anderssen
Black: B. Suhle

1 e4 e5 2 Nf3 Nc6 3 Bb5 Nge7 This is a developing move but not a good one as it blocks the bishop. **4 d4 exd4 5 0-0 Ng6 6 Nxd4 Be7 7 Nf5** As the attacking player, White wishes to avoid exchanges. You need pieces to attack with! **7...0-0 8 Nc3 Bc5 9 Qh5** This move would not be possible if the black knight had developed to f6 on move 3. **9...d6 10 Bg5** White now has five pieces developed to Black's three, with three white pieces around the black king. **10...Qe8?** 10...f6 was better. (diagram) **11 Nxg7 Kxg7??** Black should play 11...Qe5, attacking the knight and pinning the bishop. **12 Qh6+** Now Black must play 12...Kg8 and after 13 Bf6 there is no way to prevent 14 Qg7 mate. **White resigned.**

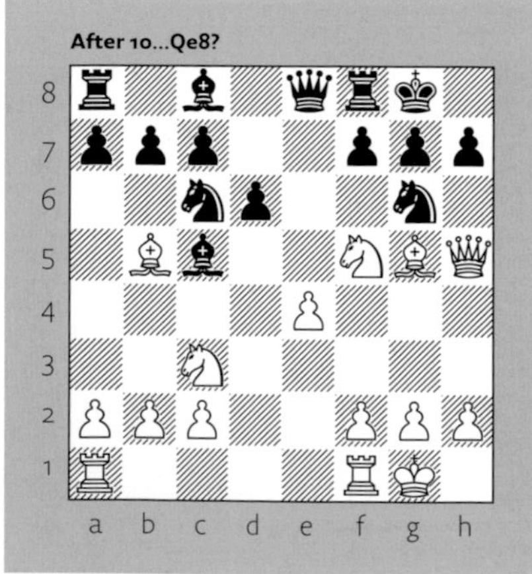

Paul Morphy (1837–84)

Paul Morphy was a child chess prodigy, born in New Orleans to a rich family. He is one of the greatest players of all time and, for the brief period when he was active as a player, he demonstrated that he was head and shoulders above all his contemporaries by displaying an insight into the game which no-one else would have for several decades.

He emerged from the South to play in the first American Championship in New York in 1857, which he easily won. Morphy then embarked on a prolonged visit to Europe during which he defeated every player of note, except Howard Staunton (see opposite) who never played against him.

By 1860 Morphy had given up competitive chess and wished to practice law, but no-one would give legal work to a mere chess player.

ABOVE: Paul Morphy, 'the pride and sorrow of chess', had a brief but brilliant career.

White: P. Morphy
Black: Count Issard and the Duke of Brunswick
(see diagram)

10 Nxb5! cxb5 11 Bxb5+! 11 Bd5 would also win the game. **11...Nbd7** Now both black knights are pinned. **12 0-0-0** threatening to take the d7-knight, for nothing. **12...Rd8 13 Rxd7 Rxd7** Now the rook is pinned instead. Attack it! **14 Rd1 Qe6** Unpinning the knight and hoping to exchange queens. But White has a brilliant finish. **15 Bxd7+** A bishop fork. **15...Nxd7 16 Qb8+!** Opening the d-file. **16...Nxb8** The only move. **17 Rd8 mate.**

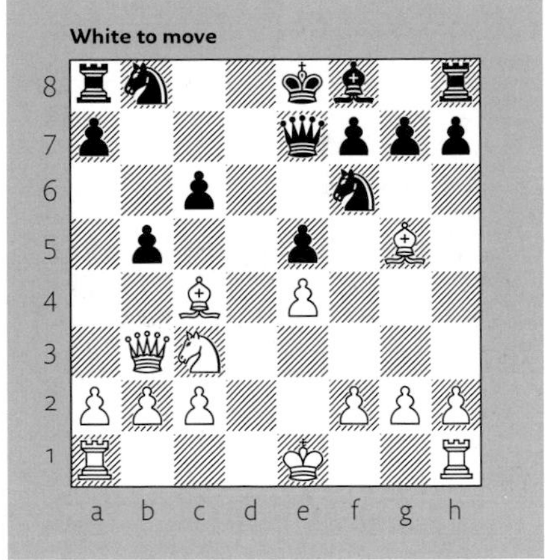

ABOVE: **Wilhelm Steinitz, the first World Champion and a major contributor to the theory of the game.**

Wilhelm Steinitz (1836–1900)

Born in Prague, Steinitz went to study in Vienna in 1858 and travelled to London to play in the international tournament of 1862. He remained in London, which was then the centre of the chess world. He defeated Adolf Anderssen (see page 162) in 1866 and Zukertort in 1886 and this latter match was the first for the Championship of the World. He lost the championship to Emanuel Lasker (see opposite) in 1894.

Steinitz moved to the USA in 1882. He wrote a number of books on the game and edited the *International Chess Magazine* from 1885–91.

One of the most profound thinkers on the game, Steinitz used his magazine to propound his views and explain his ideas. It is still an illuminating read.

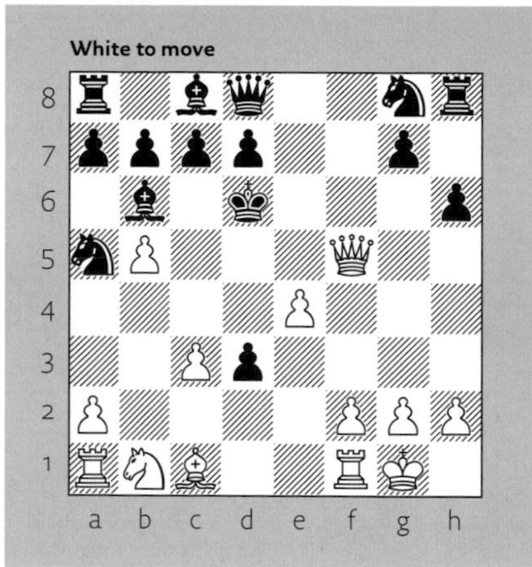

White: W. Steinitz
Black: Holstein
(see diagram)

13 e5+ Neither of the bishop checks work. **13...Ke7** If the king goes forwards, it is sure to be checkmated. **14 Ba3+ d6** 14...c5? is answered by 15 bxc6+ (*en passant* with discovered check!) 15...d6 16 Bxd6+ Ke8 17 Qf8 mate. **15 exd6+** White can ignore the threat to his queen. Now the e-file is open. **15...Ke8** After 15...cxd6, 16 Re1+ finishes the game quickly. **16 d7+!** This opens the diagonal for the bishop. 16 Re1+ would win but not so quickly. **16...Qxd7 17 Qf8 mate.**

Emanuel Lasker (1868–1941)

Born in a suburb of Berlin, Lasker entered the international arena in 1889 and won the World Championship only five years later. He dominated the chess world until the First World War in both tournament and match play. He lost his world title to Capablanca (see page 166) in 1921 but was successful in three more tournaments between 1923–25, after which he retired. He returned to competitive play in 1934–36, competing in four major tournaments with good results.

Lasker was one of the greatest players of all time – a fighter, both subtle and profound, and capable of playing with great power. He edited a number of chess magazines, wrote chess columns and books and led a wandering life, living in turn in Germany, England, the USA, Germany, the Soviet Union and the USA.

ABOVE: Emanuel Lasker, the second World Champion, was a fierce competitor who dominated the chess world from 1894–1914.

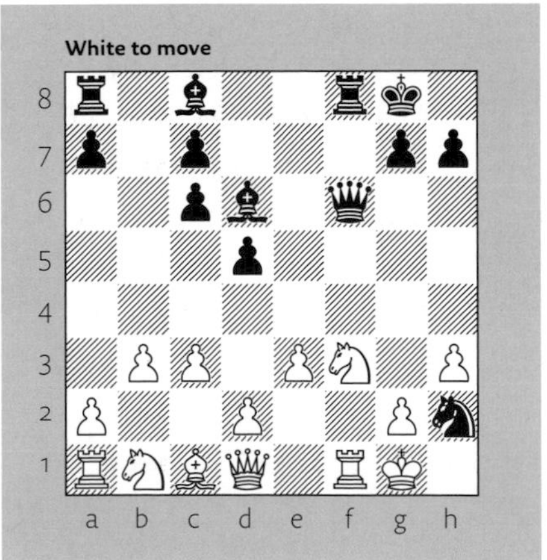

White: Reif

Black: E. Lasker

(see diagram)

This is the earliest international game we have of Lasker's. Black's knight is attacking the white rook and knight – a sort of knight fork, and also setting a trap for White. **12 Nxh2 Bxh2+** This check forces the king to desert the rook.

13 Kxh2 Qxf1 and Black is the exchange ahead and won.

ABOVE: 'Capa', the third World Champion, one of the most gifted players of all time.

José Raoul Capablanca y Graupera (1888–1942)

Born in Cuba, Capablanca was a chess prodigy but his parents didn't allow him to play much until 1901. He went to school in the USA in 1904 but spent most of his time playing chess. He beat the American Champion, Frank Marshall, in a match in 1909 to become a master and won his first international tournament in Spain in 1911. In 1913 his government employed him in their Foreign Office but with few duties, relieving him of money worries and enabling him to play chess whenever he wished.

In 1921 he defeated Lasker (see page 165) to win the World Championship which he held until 1927 when he lost to Alekhine (see opposite). He continued to play but could not secure a return match. He died in New York of a stroke.

Capablanca's style was direct and classical. He had a phenomenally quick sight of the board, faultless judgement and excelled in the ending. His chief fault was laziness.

White: Capablanca
Black: A. Pulvermacher
(see diagram)
White could play 1 Bxe8, winning the exchange but losing his e-pawn and his attack. He prefers his attack. **1 Rxa6! Bxa6 2 Rb1+ Bb7 3 Bc6** (winning the black bishop) **3...Rxe7 4 Rxb7+ Kc8 5 Ra7!** and there is no way to prevent 6 Ra8 mate.

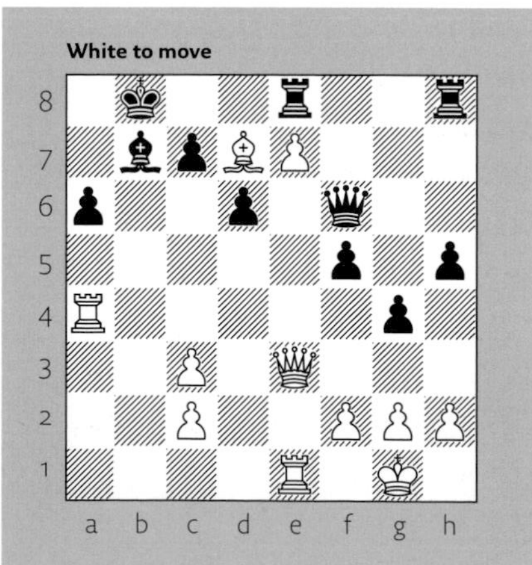

Alexander Alexandrovich Alekhine (1892–1946)

ABOVE: Alexander Alekhine (this French spelling of his name is commonly used; it is pronounced 'Alekin') was the fourth World Champion.

Alekhine was born in Moscow into a rich family and was taught chess by his mother at the age of seven. He was obsessed with the game for the rest of his life. He began playing international chess in 1908, won the Russian Championship in 1914 and qualified to play in the top class tournament in St Petersburg in the same year.

He survived the First World War and Russian Revolution, but his family lost their money. He managed to leave the Soviet Union in 1921, never to return. Steadily improving his results and reputation throughout the 1920s, he qualified to meet Capablanca for the World Championship in late 1927 and won.

He was clearly the world's best player for the next few years but his liking for drink cost him the Championship in 1935. He sobered up and regained the title in 1937 and retained it until his death, in poverty, in 1946. The extent of his collaboration with the Nazis is still argued about.

White: Alekhine
Black: A. Fletcher
(see diagram)
The white queen is under attack. **1 Qxe4! fxe4 2 Bxe4+** (White has a mating attack by 2...Kh8 3 Ng6+ Kh7 4 Nxf8+ Kh8 5 Ng6+ Kh7 6 Ne5+ Kh8 7 Nf7 mate and so Black resigned. A good demonstration of the power of discovered and double checks.

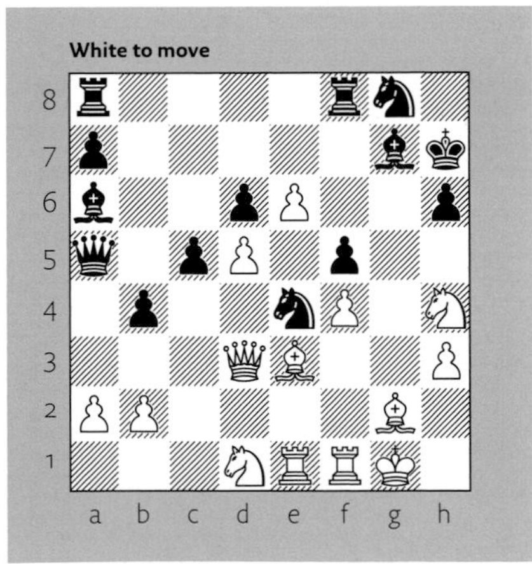

ABOVE: Max Euwe, the fifth World Champion, was active in many spheres of the game.

Machgielis (Max) Euwe (1901–81)

Euwe (pronounced 'Erva') was born in Amsterdam and was taught chess by his mother when he was four. He began to play in tournaments when he was ten and became Dutch Champion in 1921.

He was a mathematics teacher and therefore an amateur and his opportunities to play were restricted to school holidays. However, he made steady progress throughout the 1920s and early 1930s and played Alekhine for the world title in 1935, and won. He granted Alekhine (see page 167) a return match in 1937, and lost. His play had declined by the end of the Second World War, when international chess resumed.

He was the author of a huge number of chess books, director of the Netherlands Research Centre for Information Sciences (1958–64), a university professor on the same subject (1964–71) and president of FIDE (the world chess federation, 1970–78).

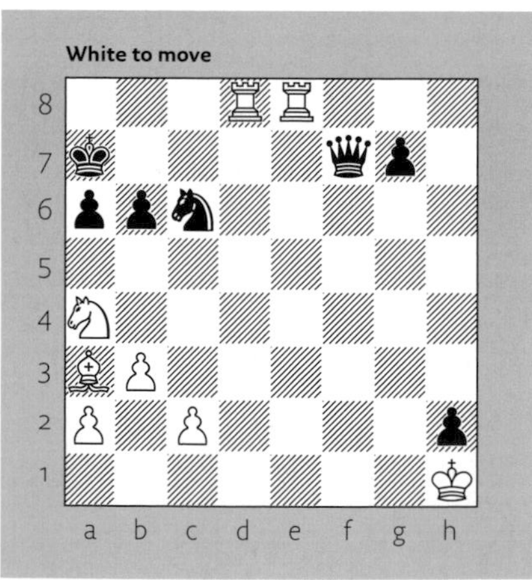

White: Euwe
Black: R. Reti
(see diagram)
White's king is wide open, so he must do something immediately. The rooks are powerful but the check on a8 leads nowhere. However, he has the seventh rank to work on. **1 Re7+! Nxe7 2 Rd7+ Ka8** (or 2...Kb8 3 Bd6+ Kc8 4 Nxb6 mate) **3 Nxb6+ Kb8 4 Bd6 mate**.

Mikhail Moiseyevich Botvinnik (1911–95)

When Alekhine (see page 167), the reigning World Champion, died in 1946, responsibility for the title was taken over by FIDE. In 1948 they organised a tournament of leading players to decide who would become Champion. The winner was Leningrad's Mikhail Botvinnik. He learned chess at the age of 12 and, under the encouragement of the Soviet State, made rapid progress. By the mid-1930s he was playing successfully at the top level.

Undoubtedly talented, he was also a tremendously hard worker, studying the game for many hours. He is said to be responsible for players adopting a professional attitude towards chess – diet, exercise, study, preparation for each game, and so on. He has several discoveries in the openings to his credit. Intense competition from other Soviet players caused him to lose the Championship three times between 1948–63, but he regained it twice.

ABOVE: Mikhail Botvinnik was the first Soviet World Champion and the last champion who was not a fulll-time player. He was also an engineer.

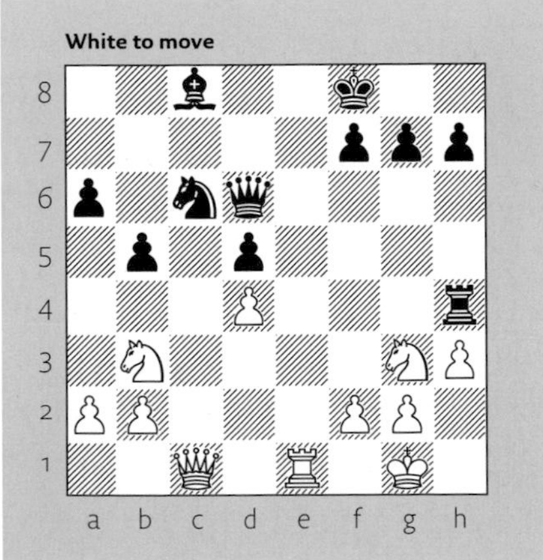

White: Botvinnik

Black: A. Havin

(see diagram)

White wishes to attack e7 but must first remove the black knight and queen that are defending it. **1 Na5!** (the black knight is pinned!) **1...Bd7 2 Nxc6 Qxc6** (if 2...Bxc6 White has the knight fork 3 Nf5) **3 Qg5! Rh6 4 Qe7+** and White mates by 4...Kg8 5 Qd8+ Be8 6 Rxe8+ Qxe8 7 Qxe8 mate.

ABOVE: Vasily Smyslov, World Champion 1957–58; the outstanding player throughout the 1950s.

Vasily Vasiliyevich Smyslov (born 1921)

Smyslov was the son of a Moscow chess player of some skill. He learned to play aged six and studied his father's chess books. He developed rapidly in the period 1935–38 and continued to improve during the Second World War. In the international arena during 1945–46, he showed himself to be a world class player.

Smyslov qualified to play Botvinnik for the world title in 1954 and drew. He qualified again in 1957 and won the title, only to lose the return match unexpectedly in 1958. He was never quite as good after this disappointment although he has continued to play in international events, with slowly declining success, well into old age.

He has edited a chess newspaper and written an autobiography and a 'best games' collection.

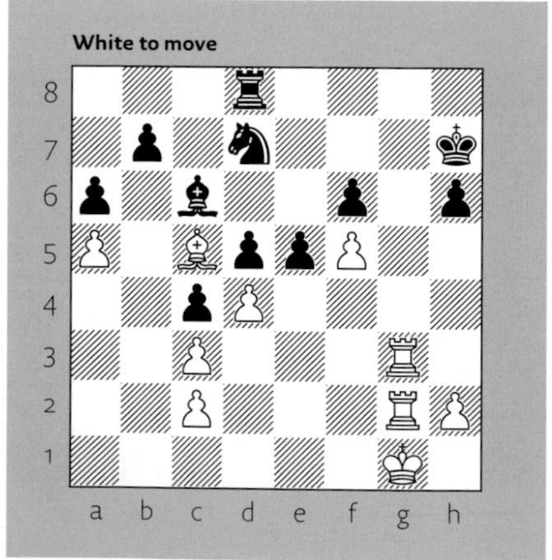

White: Smyslov

Black: I. Boleslavsky

(see diagram)

White's rooks are all powerful while Black's king has been deserted by his own pieces. White must organize a mating position. **1 Rg7+ Kh8 2 R7g6** (threatening Rxh6 mate) **2...Kh7 3 Ba3!** (White brings up his reserves) **3...exd4 4 Bc1!** and Rxh6 mate will follow.

Mikhail Nekhemyevich Tal (1936–92)

ABOVE: Mikhail Tal, World Champion 1960–61; a tactician of amazing ability whose poor health prevented him from achieving even greater success.

Born in Riga, Latvia, Tal was the son of a doctor and first encountered chess when he saw it played in his father's waiting room. He joined a chess club when he was eight and made steady progress. After winning the Latvian Championship in 1953 he made rapid progress in the many very strong Soviet events, winning the prestigious USSR Championship in 1957. He continued his meteoric rise and qualified to play Botvinnik (see page 169) for the World Championship in 1960. He won, only to lose the return match in 1961.

Tal had a deformed hand, said to be the result of a war-time accident. His health was always poor; in particular he had kidney problems and this probably led to his loss of the title in 1961. He was a tactical genius and in certain types of position was virtually impossible to play against. His record in international events was excellent especially when he was in good health. A prolific chess journalist and enthusiast , Tal was well-liked but his bohemian lifestyle was not appreciated by the Soviet authorities.

White: Tal
Black: Leonov
(see diagram)
White has four pieces close to the black king. Black has four defenders with little or no space. **1 Nf6+! Nxf6** (1...gxf6 is answered by 2 exf6 Rc7 3 Rg4+ Ng5 4 Rxg5+ hxg5 5 Qh7 mate; or if 3...Kh8 then 4 Rg7 and all is lost) **2 exf6 Rc7** (if 2...gxf6 then 3 Rxf6 followed by Rxh6 and Rh8+) **3 fxg7 Kxg7** (after 3...Qxg7 4 Rg4, Black's queen is lost) **4 Qe5+** (this fork wins the c7-rook and also mates – 4...Kg8 5 Rg4+ Qg7 6 Qxg7 mate).

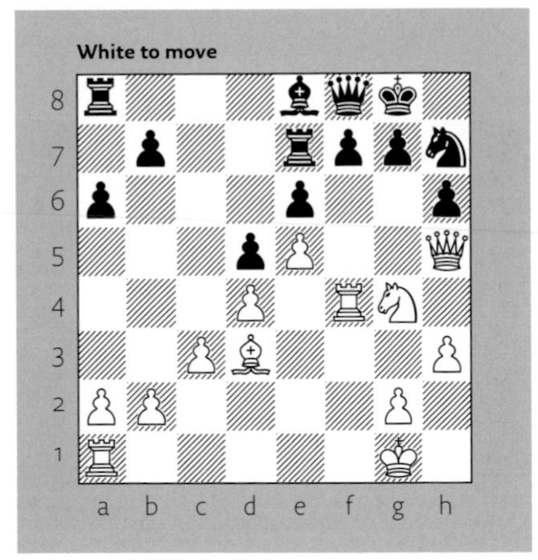

ABOVE: Tigran Petrosian, the 'solid' World Champion between 1963–69. His style of play was not popular with the fans.

Tigran Vartanovich Petrosian (1929–84)

An Armenian from Tbilisi, Petrosian learned chess when he was young. He was orphaned before he was 16 and sought solace in chess. By 1952 he had fought his way up to the top class in chess. After that his progress was slow but steady, and by the early 1960s he qualified to play Botvinnik (see page 169) for the World Championship. In 1963 he defeated Botvinnik and won the title and this time there was no return match.

Petrosian beat the next challenger, Boris Spassky (see page 173), in 1966 but lost to him the next time round in 1969. He was not a successful World Champion as he had difficulty in demonstrating his superiority. While he was champion, he played in seven tournaments and won only two (equal first in both).

After losing the Championship, Petrosian's record improved. He played in 23 major tournaments in the period 1969–80 and achieved eight first and nine second prizes. His style of play was non-committal, seeking to improve the positions of his pieces rather than seeking tactical chances. This led to many draws.

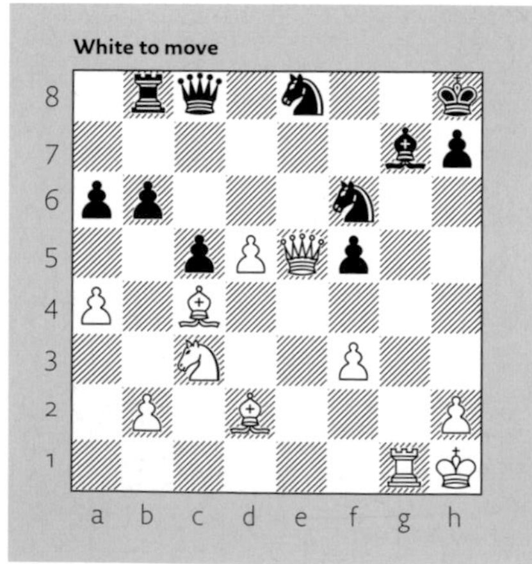

White: Petrosian
Black: L. Schmid
(see diagram)
White dominates the centre and has four pieces attacking the black king. The black queen and rook are out of play. White removes an important defender. **1 Rxg7! Kxg7 2 Qe7+ Kg6** (2...Kh8 3 d6 Ng8 4 Bxg8 Kxg8 5 Bh6 and mate on f8 or g7) **3 d6** Black resigned. After 3...Qb7 4 Qe3 (threatens mate) 4...Kg7 5 Qh6+ Kh8 6 Qf8+ and mate next move.

Boris Vasilyevich Spassky (born 1937)

Born in Leningrad, Spassky learned chess while living in the Urals during the Second World War, but returned home after the war and began playing regularly in 1947. A product of the intensive coaching system in Soviet Russia, Spassky was World Junior Champion and a top class grandmaster by the age of 18. He studied journalism at university and had many interests outside chess.

Spassky was uncomfortable within the Soviet system and later moved to France, but his main downfall in the late 1950s was a lack of ambition. He was, perhaps, a little lazy. He overcame these problems in the early 1960s and scored a string of successes that led to a world title match against Petrosian (see page 174) in 1966, which he lost by a very narrow margin.

They met again in 1969 and Spassky won. He was a popular and successful World Champion but could not withstand the onslaught from Bobby Fischer (see page 174) in 1972 and lost his title. He continued to play in international events and his last tournament victory was in 1983.

ABOVE: Boris Spassky, World Champion between 1969–72, was a product of the Soviet system but uncomfortable within it.

White: B. Larsen

Black: Spassky

(see diagram)

14...Rh1! 15 Rxh1 g2 16 Rf1. White will be happy to give the rook back if he can get rid of the g2-pawn. If 16 Rg1 Qh4+ 17 Kd1 Qh1 forces mate. **16...Qh4+ 17 Kd1 gxf1Q+** White resigned. After 18 Bxf1 Bxg4+ he is mated quickly.

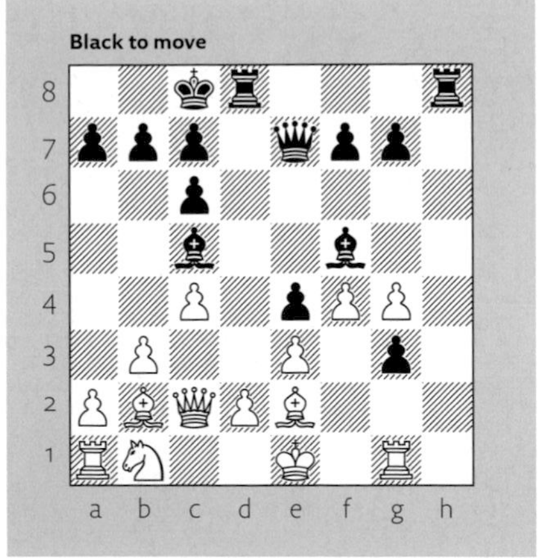

ABOVE: Bobby Fischer, World Champion between 1972–75, was the most famous and popular player of his day.

Robert James (Bobby) Fischer (born 1943)

Soviet control of the world title was sensationally broken at Reykjavik in 1972 when Fischer beat Boris Spassky (see page 173). Bobby Fischer was born in Chicago but raised in Brooklyn, New York. He obtained a chess set when he was six and was immediately absorbed by the game. He made rapid progress and by 14 was both junior and senior champion of the USA. At 16 he left school and became a professional player.

Fischer, probably the best player the world had seen (up to that time), was difficult to deal with and was probably his own biggest obstacle to becoming World Champion. Delicately assisted by an American organiser, he smashed all the other challengers in 1971 and was kept on track to a world title match in 1972. The match, in Reykjavik, captured the world's attention and despite Fischer's own attempts to jeopardise his chances by eccentric behaviour, he won easily.

Fischer didn't play again for 20 years. His title was removed in 1975 when he failed to agree terms for the match against his challenger, Anatoly Karpov (see opposite).

Fischer came out of retirement in 1992 to play a return match against Spassky, which Fischer won. He was clearly no longer playing at the same standard and since then, he has not played. He is currently living in Iceland.

White to move

White: Fischer
Black: A. di Camillo
(see diagram)
1 Bc7! (double attack, threatening the queen and the fork Re8+) **1...Nf4+** (hoping for a miracle) **2 Kf1** (there are no more checks) Black resigns.

Anatoly Yevgenyevich Karpov (born 1951)

ABOVE: Anatoly Karpov regained the World Championship for the Soviet system in 1975 and held it for ten years.

Born in Zlatoust (a small town in the Urals), Karpov learned to play aged four and was only a reasonable player at 13. He was tutored by correspondence and in summer school, and made progress. By 16, he had won a junior international tournament. At 18, he was an easy winner in the World Junior Championships, and then made very rapid progress, winning three strong tournaments out of seven in 1970–73.

In 1974 he became the official challenger for the World Championship and was awarded the title in April 1975. Over the next two years he won seven tournaments. He defended his title in 1978 and 1981 and was almost unbeatable in tournaments, establishing an outstanding record. He eventually lost the title to Kasparov (see page 176) in 1985, but was still able to improve his play, even though he could not match the new 'boy wonder'.

Karpov plans his game according to strategy and logic, regardless of his opponent. He continues to play but in recent events his results have begun to decline.

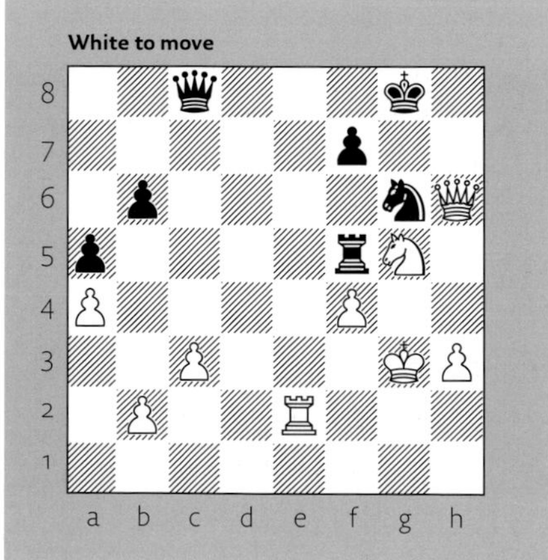

White: Karpov

Black: N. Krogius

(see diagram)

Black's king is clearly in trouble but at the moment, White only has a check. He does, however, have another approach, based on getting the rook into the attack.

1 Ne6! Black resigned as the only way to prevent checkmate is 1...fxe6 and after 2 Qxg6+ and 3 Rxe6 Black is three pawns down and likely to be mated.

ABOVE: Garry Kasparov was World Champion from 1985 until 2000. Perhaps the best player of all time, he has dominated the chess world for over 25 years.

Garry Kimovich Kasparov (born 1963)

Garry Kasparov was born in Baku, Azerbaijan, USSR with the name Harry Weinstein. The Soviets changed his name to the Russian sounding Kasparov.

He followed the Soviet training system and at the age of 12 he was Azerbaijan Champion and the USSR Under 18 Champion. He won his first international tournament in 1979 and in 1980 the World Junior Championship. A string of successes followed resulting in him becoming the official challenger for the World Championship, which he won in 1985.

Kasparov is probably the strongest player of all time with a huge list of successes to his name. Something of a rebel, he was not considered reliable by the Soviets who preferred the steady Karpov (see page 175), but Kasparov prevailed anyway. Their personal rivalry continued, but Kasparov managed to hold his title until 2000 when he lost to Kramnik.

Kasparov had predicted that Kramnik would succeed him and it is possible that this put him in the wrong frame of mind to play the younger Russian. Kasparov has recently announced his retirement from international chess.

Black to move

8 7 6 5 4 3 2 1

a b c d e f g h

White: J. Ehlvest
Black: Kasparov

(see diagram) White's queen is pinned, but so is the black rook! White's king is exposed and Black is to move, which is all Kasparov needs. **1...Qd1+** (double attack). White cannot play Qxd1 because his queen is pinned, so 2 Kg2 Qxg4+ cannot be prevented. White resigns.

Vladimir Borisovich Kramnik (born 1975)

Kramnik was born in Moscow and learned chess at the age of five. By the time he was 12 his talent was obvious and he was being encouraged. He made good progress and won the World Junior Championship at 16.

As early as 1992, Kasparov said that Kramnik was a 'brilliant talent'. He has a long list of tournament and match victories to his credit and he succeeded in winning the world title from Kasparov at the end of 2000. He has continued to be successful, but has not shown the dominance over his peers that Kasparov demonstrated. His style is quieter; he is more likely to draw, but he is exceptionally difficult to defeat.

These characteristics are more suited to match play than to tournaments and that will make it hard for anyone to take the title from him. He defended it successfully in early 2005.

ABOVE: Vladimir Kramnik (right), World Champion from 2000 to the present day, receives a trophy from British grandmaster, Ray Keene.

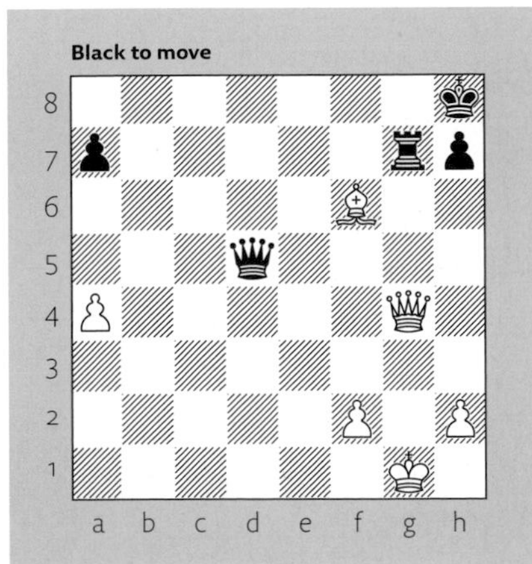

White: A. Kveinys

Black: Kramnik

(see diagram)

Positions like this are difficult because there are too many moves to choose between. Here, the odd position of the white king is the key. Kramnik finds a simple and clear path to mate. **1...Qh5+** White resigned because of 2 Ke6 Qxe5+ 3 Kf7 Qe7 mate.

First ladies

The Women's World Championship was first played in London in 1927 when Vera Menchik gave it status. After her, the standard declined but has made a major leap forward in recent years.

ABOVE: Vera Menchik was the Women's World Champion from 1927-44.

Vera Francevna Menchik (1906-44)

Vera Menchik was the first Women's World Champion. She won the title in London in 1927, held the title on every occasion until 1939 and was killed by a bomb in 1944. She dominated women's chess in that period.

Born in Moscow to a Czechoslavakian father and an English mother, she learned to play at the age of nine. In 1921 Menchik came to live in England, where she was coached by the Hungarian grandmaster Maroczy, who was living temporarily in Hastings.

She was a positional player who competed in men's international events but with only modest success. She married the Englishman Rufus Stephenson in 1937 and is sometimes known by her married name.

White: Menchik
Black: G.Thomas
(see diagram)
18 Nf5+! Nxf5 18...Bxf5 was slightly better. 18...gxf5 19 gxf5+ would leave the black king too exposed. **19 gxf5 a3 20 f6+! Kh8** If 20...Kxf6, 21 Qg5 is mate. **21 Qh6** threatens Qg7 mate. **21...axb2+ 22 Kb1** This is simplest. If 22 Kxb2, Black has checks. **22...Rg8 23 hxg6 fxg6 24 Qxh7+!** Black resigns because of 24...Kxh7 25 Rh1+ Bh3 26 Rxh3 mate.

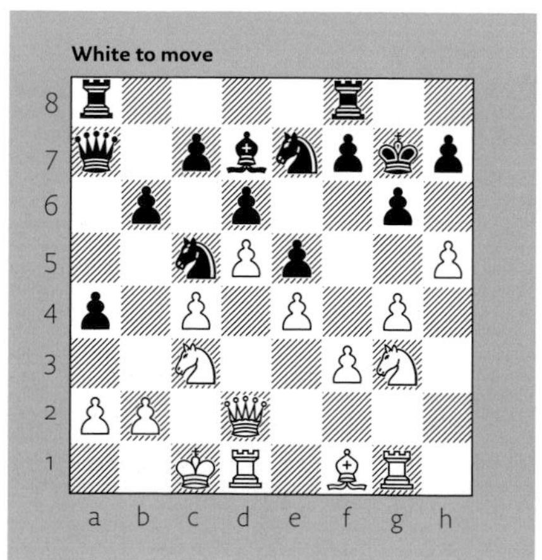

Judit(h) Polgar (born 1976)

Judit Polgar is the youngest of three Hungarian sisters, the daughters of a chess master who brought them up to be chess players. For most of their careers, their father refused to allow them to play against other women, believing that they needed the tougher practice they would get against male players. It seems to have worked.

The oldest sister, Zsuzsa (Susan; born 1969) did eventually play against other women and won the Women's World Championship. Judit has continued to play only against men and is now a formidable player, having recently been ranked tenth in the world.

She is significantly better than all other current women players and is a threat to any opponent. Unlike many women players, she has an aggressive, tactical style.

ABOVE: Judit Polgar is easily the best woman player of all time, but has never played for the Women's World Championship.

White: J. Polgar

Black: V. Anand

(see diagram) A truly remarkable combination finishes the game. The white queen is attacked. **55 f4! exf4** Now the long black diagonal is open. **56 Rh8+** Here, Black resigned. He might have allowed the spectators to see the rest! 56...Kg7 57 Qd4+ Bf6 58 Qxf6+!! Rxf6 59 Rh7+! Kxh7 60 Nxf6+ Kg7 61 Nxd7 and White wins easily. Magic!

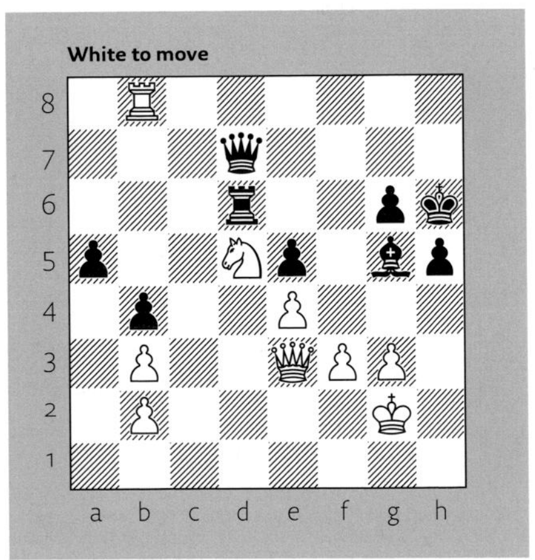

Grandmasters

There are a few words connected with chess that everyone has heard – check, checkmate and grandmaster are the most common. The first two have already been explained.

In 1838, a correspondent to an English newspaper described a British chess writer as a 'grand master'. Some years later, other writers, looking back on the career of François-André Danican Philidor (see page 160), also referred to him by that title.

In the early 20th century, some of the top international tournaments were called 'grandmaster events' and it is probably from this period that the name became more common and its usage was settled as meaning 'the top players'. In 1950, the World Chess Federation (FIDE) began awarding titles to players. They created two titles for players, International Master and International Grandmaster and

BELOW: Boris Spassky (right) begins his fight for the World Championship against Tigran Petrosian.

LEFT: Garry Kasparov defends his title unsuccessfully against Vladimir Kramnik.

they have since added a third, FIDE Master, extending the lower end of the scale.

Later, FIDE adopted an international grading system which calculates player's performances in international events and which also sets qualification standards for achieving the three FIDE titles. Under this system a FIDE Master is a player who achieves results of approximately 2,300 grading points. The International Master level is 2,400 points and International Grandmasters are expected to play at the 2,500 standard.

The number of grandmasters has risen sharply in recent years and now stands at over 200. Those who achieve a rating over 2,600 are considered to be world class players; the small number rated over 2,700 are the world elite. Only three players (Fischer, Karpov and Kasparov) have managed to achieve results averaging over 2,800 in a year and maintaining such a standard seems to be almost impossible.

Glossary

Attack: an attacking piece threatens to take an enemy piece
Back rank mate: a mate delivered by a rook or queen along the 1st or 8th rank (see page 155)
Backward pawn: any pawn which is behind its own pawns on adjacent files; such a pawn is weak because it can only be protected by a piece
Bad bishop: a weak bishop with reduced mobility because it is blocked by its own pawns
Bad move: a move which gives away material without adequate compensation or which leads to a worsening of the position
Bishop: the piece which moves on diagonals and is worth between 3 and 3+ points
Board: a chess board has eight rows of eight squares, coloured alternately black and white – the board must be placed so that there is always a white square in the bottom right-hand corner
Capture: when a piece is taken and removed from the board
Castling: a move with the king and rook, simultaneously, designed to remove the king from the centre, where it is often in danger, and to bring the rook into more active play
Centre: the four squares in the middle of the board which are important because most pieces are at their strongest when placed there
Check: any move which threatens a king
Checkmate: a check from which a king cannot escape that wins the game
Defend: a piece is defended if, should it be captured, the capturing piece can itself be taken
Development: bringing pieces into active play
Diagonal: a line of squares on the board of the same colour

Discovered check: when one piece moves, revealing a check from another piece

Double attack: when a piece moves and attacks an enemy piece and the move also reveals a second attack, from another piece, on a different enemy piece

Double check: when a piece moves, giving check, but also revealing a check from a second piece

Doubled pawn: two pawns on the same file; they are usually weak, especially when they are isolated, doubled pawns and particularly if they are on a half-open file; it is possible to have tripled pawns but this is very rare

Doubled rooks: when one side has both of its rooks on the same file; this is often very powerful

Doubled rooks on the 7th (2nd) rank: when one side has both rooks deep in the enemy position on the 7th or 2nd rank, they usually have a won game

En passant: a special pawn capture that is explained on pages 23–4

The exchange: the difference between a rook and a knight or a rook and a bishop – a player who wins a rook for a knight (or bishop) is said to have 'won the exchange' (i.e. the piece of higher value)

Exchanges: when one side captures and the other recaptures, they are said to have 'exchanged' pieces (the term implies that the captured pieces are of equal value)

Felted pieces: chess pieces with cloth (felt) on the bottom to make them quiet when moved

FIDE: the international ruling body of chess – Fédération Internationale des Échecs

FIDE Master: the lowest category of international player (see page 181)

File: a line of squares on a chess board which runs from one player to the other; such lines are lettered a–h from White's left

Fool's Mate: the shortest mate possible in chess (see page 110)

Fork: a simultaneous attack on two or more pieces
Gambits: a name given to openings where one side gives up material in order to gain some other advantage such as an attack, control of the centre, faster development, etc.
Good move: a move which gains material or which improves the position
Grandmaster: the highest rank of international player (see pages180–1)
Half-open file: any file which has a pawn or pawns on it from one side only; such a file will often be occupied by the other side's rooks
Initiative: the side that is dictating the play has the initiative, which can range from the very small to something large enough to win the game
International master: the middle ranking of international players (see pages 180–1)
Isolated pawn: a pawn which does not have a pawn of the same colour on an adjacent file – it is usually weak as it must be defended by a piece
King: the weakest piece on the board; usually with no value; the object of the game is to attack and capture it
King's side: the half of the board on which the kings begin the game – files e–h
Knight: the chess piece with the strangest way of moving and worth between 3 and 3+ points (see pages 40–5)
Minor pieces: knights and bishops
Major pieces: queens and rooks
Open file: any file which has no pawn on it; these are important because they are potential highways into the opponent's (or your!) position
Opposite coloured bishops: when each side has only one bishop and they move on different coloured squares, they have 'opposite coloured bishops'; when only those bishops and pawns are left, the chance of a draw is very high

Passed pawn: a pawn that does not have to get passed an opponent's pawn in order to promote; they are potentially very dangerous

Pawn: the weakest attacking piece, usually worth 1 point

Pawn majority: this occurs when a player has more pawns than his opponent in one area of the board

Pawn promotion: when a pawn reaches the far side of the board it is 'promoted'; it immediately becomes a queen, rook, bishop or knight as its player chooses

Perpetual check: a series of checks which can continue forever - a way of drawing a game

Pieces: this term is used in two different ways; sometimes it refers to queens, rooks, bishops and knights, but sometimes the pawns are also included

Pin: something which restricts the movement of a piece, either partially or totally (see pages 96–9)

Protected passed pawn: a passed pawn which benefits from the protection of another pawn; potentially very powerful in the endgame

Protection: when one piece defends another, it 'protects' it

Queen: the strongest piece on the chess board, worth about 9 points

Queen's side: the half of the board on which the queens begin the game - files a–d

Rank: a line of squares which runs across the board between the players - ranks are numbered 1–8

Recapture: when one side takes an enemy piece and the opponent captures back on the next move

Repetition of moves: a method of drawing a game in which both sides repeat their moves; a sort of perpetual check without the checks

Rook: the chess piece which moves along ranks and files and is worth about 5 points

Rook on the 7th (2nd) rank: a rook which has penetrated the opponent's position almost to their back rank; such a rook is usually a very powerful piece

Sacrifice: giving up material in order to gain an advantage in position, such as a strong attack

Scholar's Mate: a simple checkmate often seen in school chess (see page 111)

Skewer: an attack by one piece on two enemy pieces that stand on the same straight line – this can lead to a gain in material

Smothered Mate: a checkmate delivered to a king which is surrounded by its own pieces (see page 156)

Stalemate: when the side to move does not have a legal move and is not in check, it is stalemate and the game is drawn

Threat: the intention to play an advantageous move if the opponent doesn't prevent it

United passed pawns: two or more passed pawns on adjacent files – they are very powerful

Weighted pieces: chessmen with a piece of lead inserted into their base to make them harder to knock over, are said to be 'weighted' or 'loaded'

Need to know more?

Now you have read this book and learned how the pieces move and what the game is about, you may have some idea how important chess will be to you. So far you have only taken the first few steps and need now to decide what to do next.

Knowing how the pieces move is barely even an introduction to the game. The important thing now is to play and play and play. You need to become so familiar with the moves of the pieces and the ideas behind threats, captures, check and checkmate that they become instinctive.

Practice

Find an opponent, preferably someone who will be around often enough for you to play them regularly and get playing. Plenty of people watch the top players compete against one another, but most players prefer to play.

If you cannot find an opponent, then a chess playing computer is the next best thing. This can be a piece of software

LEFT: Outdoor play with giant-sized chess pieces and board can be found in parks and public places throughout the world.

that runs on your normal computer or it may be a dedicated chess playing machine. In both cases, you will usually be able to set them to play at different levels. Choose the lowest level and start playing. Once you can beat the 'machine' most of the time, move it up a level and try again.

Books

Another approach, which has worked for generations of players, is to turn to chess books. It is important to choose a book which was first published in the last ten years or so. English language chess books before that were often published with a different method of writing the moves to the one given in this book. You won't find them easy to understand.

You should choose a book on tactics or on miniature games (these are games with 25 moves or fewer). If they aren't available, then a collection of games will probably suit you. Ignore the comments on the moves and concentrate on playing through the games. Most libraries have a good selection of chess books.

Correspondence play

For many years, chess has been played by post. There is now an international body, the International Correspondence Chess Association (ICCA) which organises competitions for the correspondence world championship and world team championship. There are several correspondence chess clubs in the UK and you can find them via links on www.chessmail.com. This is not a suitable form of chess for beginners but some of the clubs may offer competitions for relative novices, once you get that far.

Correspondence chess is especially useful for players who live in isolated places, work difficult hours or who cannot get to ordinary chess clubs for other reasons.

Clubs

One of the problems that beginners face is that chess clubs do not generally cater for them (except school chess clubs). Your local library may have a list of chess clubs in your area and once you have got past the novice stage, they will be very pleased to see you.

Magazines

The major chess magazines in English are:

British Chess Magazine (www.bcmchess.co.uk) based in London

Chess (www.chess.co.uk) also based in London

Chess Life (www.uschess.org) published by the United States Chess Federation

New in Chess (www.newinchess.com) published in the Netherlands.

The internet

There is also a web publication, The Week in Chess (TWIC), which can be accessed through the www.chess.co.uk site. TWIC covers the international chess scene, giving huge collections of games played in major international events from all over the world. Of course, all of these sites have links to other chess sites. You can visit sites run by the organisers of major tournaments and watch the tournament being played via your computer, in real time. The site is updated every time someone makes a move. There are usually between five and eight games being played at once, so there is quite a lot to keep up with.

Index

A

Alekhine, Alexander Alexandrovich 167
Anand, V. 179
Anderssen, Adolf 162

B

back rank mate 155
backward pawn 150
bishop 25–9
  bad bishop 155
Boleslavsky, I. 170
Botvinnik, Mikhail Moiseyevich 169

C

Capablanca y Graupera, José Raoul 166
castling 64–5
centre, the 140–1
champion players 160–79
check 51–7
  defend with check 131
  discovered check 58
  double check 59, 95
  winning ways with check 93–4
checkmate 61–2
  forcing checkmate 102, 106–7
checkmate threats 81
chess boards 10–12
  board direction 13
  setting up the board 15
  size of board 13
chess etiquette 51
chess punctuation marks 72
chess sets 10–12
combination 147
Count Issard 163
counter attack 135

D

de Segura, Ruy Lopez
defending (tactics) 130–7
  defend with a double attack 136
  defend with a fork 134
  defend with a mate threat 132
  defend with a pin 133
  defend with a skewer 135
  defend with check 131
development 142–3
di Camillo, A. 174
diagonal 13
discovered check 58
double attacks 91–2
  defend with a double attack 136
double check 59, 95
doubled pawns 149
doubled rooks 153
doubled rooks on the 7th (2nd) rank 154
Duke of Brunswick 163

E

Ehlvest, J. 176
en passant 23–4
endgame 102–3
Euwe, Machgielis (Max) 168
Exchange, the 147
exchanges 74–5, 79–80

F

file 13
Fischer, Robert James (Bobby) 174, 181
Fletcher, A. 167
Fool's Mate 111
foot soldiers 16
forks 84–9
  defend with a fork 134

G

gambits 145
Game and Playe of the Chesse, The 8
grandmaster 180–1

H

Havin, A. 169
Hostein 164

I

Illustrated London News 161
initiative, the 143–4
isolated pawn 149

K

Karpov, Anatoly Yevgenyevich 175, 181
Kasparov, Garry Kimovich 176, 181
king 46–50
knight 40–5
Kramnik, Vladimir Borisovich 177
Krogius, N. 175
Kveinys, A. 177

L

Lasker, Emanuel 165
Leonov

M

Maroczy 178
Menchik, Vera Francevna 178
middlegame 100–1
Morphy, Paul 163

N

notation 72–3

O

open file/half-open file 145–6

opposite coloured bishops 154
origins of chess 8–9

P
pawn 16–21
isolated pawn 149
passed pawn 148
pawn majority 152
pawn promotion 22, 104
perpetual check 157
Petrosian, Tigran Vartanovich 172
Philidor, François-André Danican 160
Pierre St-Amant 161
pins 96–9
defend with a pin 133
Polgar, Judit(h) 179
protected passed pawn 152
protecting pieces 76–8
Pulvermacher, A. 166

Q
queen 35–9

R
rank 13
reading and writing chess 72–3
Reif 165
repetition of moves 157
Reti, R. 168
rook 30–4
rook on the 7th (2nd) rank 153

S
sacrifice 146
Schmid, L. 172
Scholar's Mate 111
short games 110–25
simple defences 130
skewers 90
defend with a skewer 135
Smothered Mate 156
Smyslov, Vasily Vasiliyevich 170
Spassky, Boris Vasilyevich 173
stalemate 63
Staunton, Howard 161
Staunton pattern 161
Steinitz, Wilhelm 164
Suhle, B. 162

T
Tal, Mikhail Nekhemyevich 171
Thomas, G. 178

U
united passed pawns 151
unprotected pieces 128–9

V
values of the pieces 68–71

W
weighted pieces 11
Women's World Championship 178–9
World Chess Championship 159
World Chess Federation (FIDE) 159, 180
World Team Championship 159

Acknowledgements

The chess equipment used in the original photography was kindly loaned by BCM Chess Shop (www.bcmchess.co.uk)

Picture credits

All original studio photography by George Morse (©m&n publishing)

Thanks also to the following for providing photographs for the book:

British Chess Magazine 161, 162,163, 164, 165, 166, 167, 168, 169, 170, 171, 172, 173, 174, 177, 179, 180, 181
British Library 9
Chessgraphics 8
Corbis 178
Getty Images 175, 176
Laima Barkus (©m&n publishing) 187
Lee Sharman (©m&n publishing) 12

Collins need to know?

Look out for these recent titles in Collins' practical and accessible need to know? series.

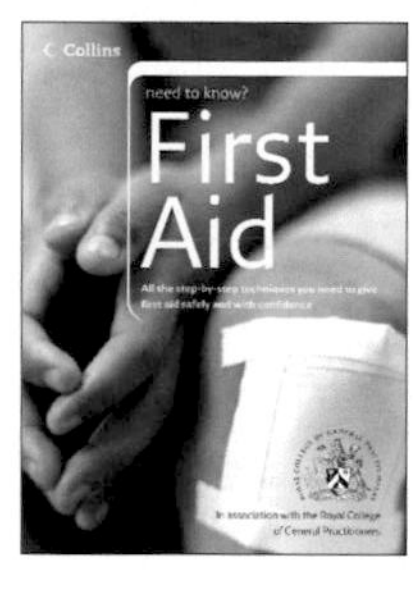

Other titles in the series:

Antique Marks
Birdwatching
Body Language
Buying Property in France
Card Games
DIY
Dog Training
Drawing & Sketching
Golf
Guitar
How to Lose Weight
Kama Sutra
Kings and Queens
Knots
Low GI/GL Diet
Pilates
Poker
Speak French
Speak Italian
Speak Spanish
Stargazing
Watercolour
Weddings
Woodworking
The World
Yoga
Zodiac Types

To order any of these titles, please telephone 0870 787 1732 quoting reference 263H.
For further information about all Collins books, visit our website: www.collins.co.uk